Fabric of ENDURANCE

© 2019 by TGS International, a wholly owned subsidiary of Christian Aid Ministries, Berlin, Ohio.

All rights reserved. No part of this book may be used, reproduced, or stored in any retrieval system, in any form or by any means, electronic or mechanical, without written permission from the publisher except for brief quotations embodied in critical articles and reviews.

ISBN: 978-1-949648-59-1

Cover and text layout design: Kristi Yoder

Printed in the USA

Published by:

TGS International
P.O. Box 355
Berlin, Ohio 44610 USA
Phone: 330.893.4828
Fax: 330.893.2305
www.tgsinternational.com

TGS001895

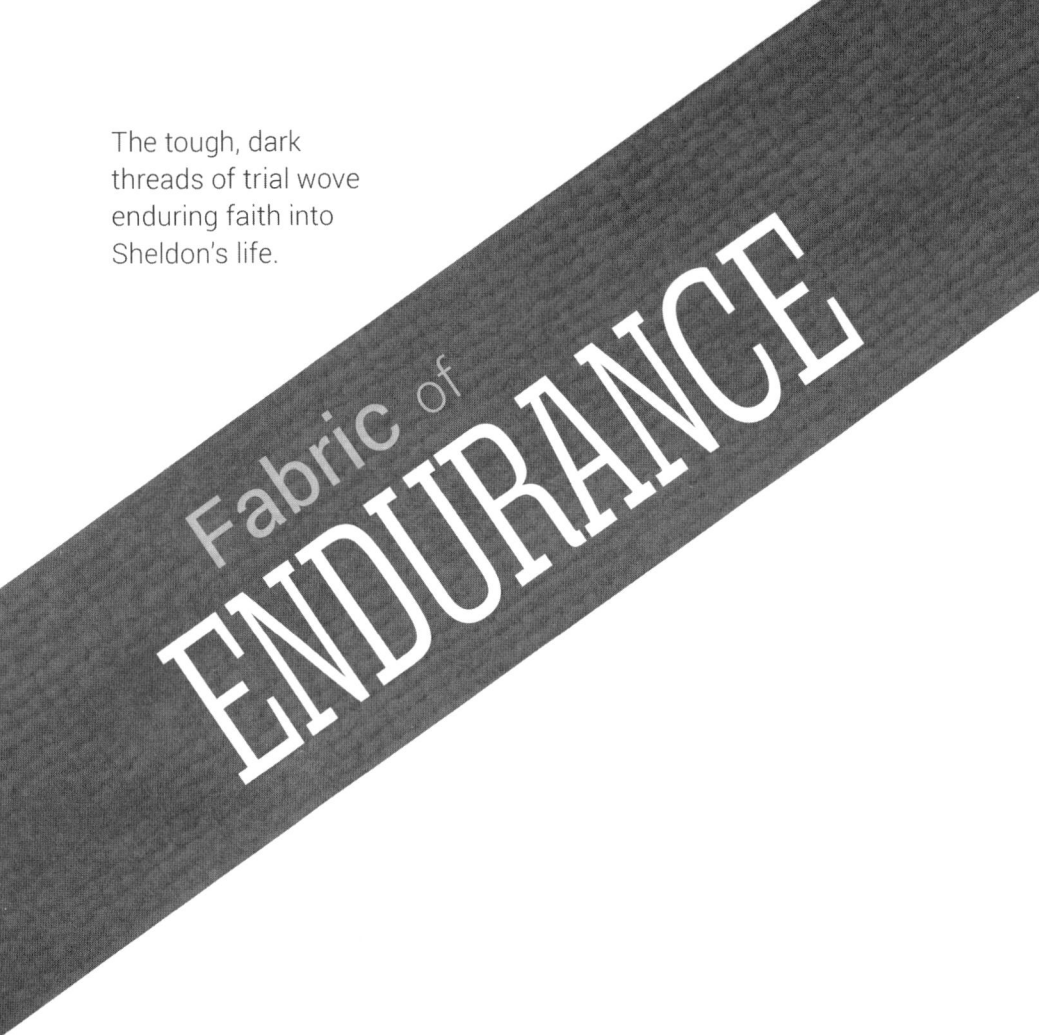

The tough, dark threads of trial wove enduring faith into Sheldon's life.

Fabric of ENDURANCE

Harold R. Troyer

CONTENTS

1. A Christmas Child 7
2. Depression Days 13
3. God's Way Is Perfect 25
4. A Thanksgiving Ceremony 33
5. Half Dome or Bust 43
6. No Casual Dating 51
7. Two Shall Be One 65
8. CPS Camp Days 75
9. Shadow of Death 83
10. Changing Times 95
11. "Though He Slay Me" 101
12. More Precious Than Gold 111
13. "I Can Do All Things" 117
14. Another Obstacle Conquered 125
15. A Purpose to Live 131
16. B&B Trucking 139
17. One More Answered Prayer 147
18. Aunt Frieda 157
19. Loved and Lost 161
20. "Yet Will I Trust Him" 169
21. To Grow a Garden 175
22. Beyond the Sierras 181
23. First in Worship 187
24. Accidents Aren't Planned 193
25. "Will the Circle Be Unbroken?" 199
    Epilogue 203
    About the Author 205

Three chicken houses.

Home of Sheldon and Mary Ellen.

Egg-packing house which was later remodeled for Sheldon to live in.

chapter one
A CHRISTMAS CHILD

1921

A tall, slender woman walked swiftly in the darkness. A blustery evening wind stirred bare branches and a few lonely leaves on the trees along a silent gravel road. Palm trees shivered in the cold night air. Christmas Day was giving way to night, and soon it would be just another winter day in central California.

At this time of year, the weather was comparable to a Mediterranean climate. Rainfall stimulated the growth of greener grass along the roads and in the hills. During the hot dry summer and fall, a constant breeze would dry out the landscape and kick up a fine dust. But tonight the late evening temperature dipped to near freezing, just as it did on every other winter day in the San Joaquin Valley.

The San Joaquin Valley had been home to the Yokut Indians until the Spanish explorers arrived. It had been a lush expanse of marsh and grasslands that provided food and cover for Tule elk, pronghorn antelope, mule deer, and an abundance of small game. Until less than a hundred years earlier, the Yokut Indians had lived off the land and hunted game. However, the white man came with his new diseases and his relentless greed, all but exterminating the original food sources as well as the native people. Slowly, the valley developed into fields of waving grain and, farther to the south, patches of puffy cotton. The marshes also, with their unique fauna and flora, gradually disappeared as canals were built to contain the water and the land was leveled for farming. Little towns sprang up in this new landscape and Modesto, California, in Stanislaus County lay at the heart of it all.

The tall woman walked briskly along Modesto's quiet Shoemake Avenue, her head bent against the wind and moisture. As she neared her destination, she slowed a bit to catch her breath. Not much could be seen in the dark save a distant house or two where the lights had not yet been extinguished for the night.

How many births will this make for me? she mused to herself. *And will I make it in time?* Her heartbeat quickened with her pace. She had been told only that it was time.

The sounds of her shoes on the wooden steps and her soft tapping at the door were almost lost in the gusts of wind stirring the branches above and tugging at her bonnet. However, the sturdy wooden door soon creaked open a crack as if it moved at her command. A bearded face peered through the narrow opening. The face, toughened by years of hard manual labor in the elements, displayed a tension that added to its sturdy appearance. The man's smile hinted at relief as his piercing eyes adjusted to the darkness and recognized the figure.

"Come in and unwrap," said the tall lean man. "How was your walk?" He stepped back and opened the door wide.

"I dressed warmly, so I am fine, Walter. How is Ida?"

"It sounds as though she is ready for you now. We really appreciate your prompt help. Please go to her bedroom; I will stay by the stove here in the living room." He pointed to the door across from where he stood.

Swiftly, Mary Cover picked up her bag and walked to the bedroom. A lantern hanging on a hook inside the door revealed a bed, a small table, and a wooden chair. The light played gently over the expectant mother, who was lying on the bed covered with a thin sheet. Mary set her bag on the simple wooden table and organized a few instruments she would use.

After a few hours had passed and nature's process had unfolded, a tiny boy lay swaddled in a humble patchwork quilt in his mother's arms. Mary let out a long sigh of relief. It was always a joy to be a part of the precious and intense moments of a new arrival, but the joy was mixed with apprehension and anxiety that all would turn out well. The gentle cries of the newborn filled the bedroom with an atmosphere of peace and joy that helped erase the pain the mother had experienced just moments before. *It is just as our Lord said,* thought Mary as she tidied the room, *"A woman when she is in travail hath sorrow, because her hour is come: but as soon as she is delivered of the child, she remembereth no more the anguish, for joy that a man is born into the world."*[1]

The mother peeked at the little boy beside her. A Christmas baby! He had just nursed for the first time and was sleeping soundly. A tear escaped her eye and was captured by the soft clothing wrapped around the infant. Happiness flooded her heart as she traced a finger over his face and felt his tiny hands.

"Looks like a Grover," said Walter proudly as he bent over the bed where mother and infant lay. "Welcome, Alvah Sheldon Grover."

"Shh . . . Walter," murmured his wife. "Not too loud. He needs to rest now and your voice is causing him to stir a bit. Could you ask Mary to make me a cup of hot tea with a little sugar and milk? I hear her washing something at the kitchen sink. And could you please turn off the lantern or take it with you? I need to rest."

"Sure, Ida, I can do that. Just a minute and I will be back." The wooden floor protested slightly as Walter grabbed the lantern and strode out of the room.

A cup of hot tea was steeped and ready when Walter returned from throwing a few pieces of wood onto the fire. He added a bit of sugar and milk

---

[1] John 16: 21

to the tea and stirred. The spoon tinkling against the sides of the mug kept time with the clock as it chimed midnight.

It sure is great to have neighbors like Jake and Mary Cover, Walter thought. Really, all the neighbors were a blessing to them and they wouldn't trade Modesto for anything in the world. Not even Gage County, Nebraska, which had been home to them just a few years earlier. Nebraska could just go ahead and have its blizzards, droughts, and windstorms. Walter and Ida were more inclined toward their California sunshine. Three years ago on Christmas Day they had arrived in California and now this was home. They had no intention of going anywhere else, at least not unless God had other plans. Their short move back to Kansas had cured them of any homesickness that may have been left in them for the Midwest.

Ida had become homesick for her mother and family back in Kansas, so they had rented their half of the farm to his father and packed up and left. After six months in Kansas, a terrible hailstorm devastated crops and orchards and took care of Ida's desire to stay in the familiar Midwest.

They stayed a year just to be sure of their decision before moving back to the West Coast. Now they were living in the center of Stanislaus County, California, and they were more than content. This weather was more suited for Walter's health anyway. *For anyone's health, really,* he thought.

The bedroom was quiet as Walter returned with the tea. Little Sheldon and his mother seemed to be sleeping as Walter approached the bedside.

"I'm awake," whispered Ida as her eyelids fluttered open and she gently raised herself to her elbow. She grasped the mug and took a sip. "Thank you. This is good." She settled back down beside her baby. "Did Mary leave yet?" she asked.

"I just heard the outside door open and shut, so she is probably on the way home," said Walter, scooting a chair from the little table over to the bedside.

As his companion slept, Walter sat on the wooden chair beside the bed and relaxed for a moment. The lantern from the adjoining room threw enough light through the doorway for Walter to see his wife and newborn son. What would the future hold for his little son? For his family? Life seemed normal for the most part. Lots of hard work, for sure, but that was normal for the nationals and immigrants of the San Joaquin Valley. Through working hard and eking out a living for his family, Walter had become tough. But no amount of hard work could have prepared him for the future that now awaited him with his son, his wife, and the family members who would be born.

chapter two
DEPRESSION DAYS

1927–1932

Six-year-old Sheldon shook his older brother. "Come on, Merven. Daddy said to come. Hurry and make your bed so we can go get a cup of tea before chores."

After they had a cup of tea and warmed themselves by the stove, the boys headed to the barn. The mornings were cool, so they often wore light jackets as they fed and watered the animals and gathered the eggs. By the time they were finished with their morning chores, the sun was glinting over the Sierra Mountain Range.

"Mama," Sheldon called as they banged through the kitchen doorway, "we have twenty-three eggs this morning." He set the small bucket of eggs on the kitchen floor next to the sink.

The bucket was an icon of poverty for Sheldon and his family. In the years leading up to the current year, 1927, the bucket had traveled thousands of miles across the U.S. with Sheldon's parents and grandparents. Now on

Shoemake Avenue, it was used to tote eggs, potatoes, water, and anything else a young boy needed to carry for his mother. It was a clean bucket, but over the many years and miles, it had developed a few rust spots from which the water slowly leaked out. It was worn, rusty, and squeaky—but useable all the same.

"Good," Ida said as she bustled around the kitchen preparing breakfast. "We can use more eggs this morning. We have only a few left after the custard pies I made yesterday."

Soon the family was seated at the breakfast table, where Walter offered a prayer for the morning meal. By now, the family consisted of Merven, Frieda, Sheldon, and Vera. Sheldon's stomach growled as he smelled the sausage and eggs, and he squirmed impatiently. The predawn chores, the early morning fresh air, and the wonderful smells of a piping hot breakfast made him ravenously hungry. After Daddy's prayer, their mother dished out food for the children. Things would have to keep moving along if the children were to get ready in time for the fifteen-minute walk to Ransom School. It would not look good for them to be tardy.

Sheldon took another bite of his sausage. He loved the mornings at the breakfast table with Daddy and Mama. He especially liked it when Daddy talked about the farm and the harvest. Someday he too would have a farm, with trees and grapevines and workers.

Soon the young ones were off to school. Sunshine streamed across the Grover orchard, the family's alfalfa plots, and their rows of Zinfandel grapes. Frieda and Sheldon were fortunate to begin their walk to school down the long lane that lay between acres of luscious grapevines.

Then they turned west and walked the remaining short distance on Shoemake to reach the school. Children were already milling about the school yard and talking or playing games. A few of the younger boys ran a race. A milk truck rattled up, and several children sitting on the wooden bed hopped off before it continued on to the next farm.

Secretly, Sheldon looked forward to studying. Based on all the things Daddy had been telling him about farming, he would need to learn all he could at school if he also wanted to be a successful farmer someday.

Ding-dong.

The echoing ring from the belfry announced another day of learning at Ransom School. Students pushed through the open doors and swarmed to their classrooms to begin their studies. The oiled pine floors creaked as each child found his or her assigned seat. Teachers wrote on chalkboards and greeted each student warmly.

"Good morning, boys and girls!"

"Good morning, Miss Baker."

"Psst . . . race you again at recess," Floyd mouthed. He quickly looked back to the teacher with a straight face. *Of course I will race him again,* Sheldon thought as he listened to Miss Baker's instructions. *Just like a Yokut Indian brave.* But now he needed to focus on learning.

Almost seventeen years earlier, in 1911, the original two-room building had been torn down and a new structure built with wide hallways, indoor bathrooms, a principal's office, and four new classrooms. A new bell was installed in the belfry. A coal stove heated the building on cooler days in the fall and winter. For as long as anyone could remember, Ira Grover, who lived just up the road, had been janitor.

Some students returned to Ransom School as teachers in the same classrooms they had frequented years before as children. In other cases, parents who had graduated now sent their children to the school they had attended.

/ /

A few years passed, and Sheldon continued to study diligently. He bent over his copy book and wrote down each problem carefully. Although he looked forward to graduating in a couple of years, he enjoyed his lessons, especially arithmetic. He flipped back through the book to review some of his previous assignments. He looked at a problem he had solved incorrectly and quickly found his mistake. *My grades are not as good as last year,* Sheldon thought, *but at least they are still A's and B's.*

The previous year Sheldon's teacher had suggested that he skip Grade 5 and go straight to Grade 6. "It's too easy for you," Mr. Brown had said. "You need more of a challenge. Besides," he went on, "I am sure your father could use the help on your farm, so no one will frown on you for spending one year less at school."

"Attention, class!"

Sheldon jerked and blushed as Miss Baker looked at him sternly. All eyes were on him.

"Everyone please pay attention," Miss Baker reminded them. Sheldon thought he saw a twinkle in his teacher's eye as she turned to write arithmetic problems on the board.

Don't worry, Sheldon thought. *She won't catch me dreaming again.* He sat up straight and began to follow along, computing mentally as Miss Baker's chalk scratched across the board.

As days turned into weeks and weeks into months, Sheldon tucked away all the information he could. He was developing into a fine young boy with lots of energy and dreams. He loved to research new ways of doing what used to be done with slow manual labor. Already, horses had given way to the railway, the railway had given way to the automobile, and now the age of flying machines had begun—dirigibles and airplanes. These were exciting times.

"I think I belong on the ground," Frieda said as they walked home one day. "If God wanted us in the air, He would have given us wings." She adjusted the books in her arms into a more comfortable position. "But it was interesting to watch the dirigible today and I was sure glad the teachers allowed us to go outside to see it."

"I think it would be fun to fly," Sheldon said. They had almost made their way back down the long lane to their home. It was May 18, 1932, and the dirigible, *U.S. Akron,* had caused all of Modesto to stop and watch the beautiful sight as it passed overhead at an altitude of nearly two thousand feet. Several hours later now, everyone in the small town was still talking about the giant airship and the adventures of flying.

"I would rather fly in an airplane like Charles Lindbergh." Sheldon's lively brain was always working on ideas. "A plane would give me more maneuverability and speed in the air," he said wisely. He had read recently of Lindbergh's nonstop flight across the Atlantic.

"Aw, you think you know just how it works," Vera scoffed. "How do you know about speed and that other big word you just used? Or do you just make up all this stuff?"

"Studied about it," said Sheldon with a grin. They had reached the house and he opened the screen door to the kitchen.

The kitchen was not a large room, but for now, it was big enough for Walter and Ida's immediate family. It was a simple room where the family gathered for meals and family time. Daddy would read the Bible after the evening meal and then they would wash the dishes and set them on the drain board to dry. Sometimes they sang a hymn and the children worked on schoolbooks or read an interesting story. If it was a summer evening when the light lingered, Walter would find something to do on the farm and the boys might help.

"Hi, children." Mama greeted them with a smile as she flipped fresh bread from a pan onto the counter. "Did you see the dirigible today?"

"Yes," said Vera. "We had fun running outside to see it."

"I am sure you did," Mama said, smiling slightly. "It seemed to create quite a bit of excitement everywhere. Even Grandpa and Grandma were amazed to see something that big up in the air."

"It was thoughtful of the teachers to let us go out and see it," Frieda said as she placed her books on the table. "They even gave us a little extra time to sit in groups and talk afterward. It made for a pleasant day."

"Mama," Sheldon said, "where's Pop?" Now that Sheldon was no longer a little boy, he had taken to referring to his father as Pop. He dropped his dinner pail, a leftover lard container with a lid, beside the counter where it sat when it wasn't being used. Pop had said they must use what they had these days. "We need to tighten our belts and make it do. Just be glad you get a lunch of any kind." He had read in the *Modesto News* that farmers in Oklahoma were losing their land to the banks and had to live in "Hoovervilles" made of cardboard boxes, scrap tin, old glass, or anything else that would help in making a crude shelter. A Hooverville was one of the shanty towns homeless people in the U.S. built throughout the Great Depression. They were named after Herbert Hoover. As President during the early Depression days, Hoover was often blamed for people losing their homes as well as other hardships that plagued the country during those times.

"Just be glad we have a roof over our heads and two or three square meals a day," Walter had said in his brusque way. "We need to be grateful for what we do have and be willing to share when we can."

"Pop's out in the orchard," Mama replied now as she covered the freshly baked bread with a clean towel. "He's probably out irrigating the orchard since it hasn't rained for a while. You could go check."

"Thanks, Mama," Sheldon said as he sprinted out the door for the orchard and the great outdoors he loved so well. If only he could always be out in the sunshine and wind. He would love to live just like the San Joaquin Yokut Indians of years past.

/ /

"Pop," Sheldon asked, pointing at a group of people camped along the Tuolumne River. "What are they up to?" The site was trashy, and pieces of canvas were draped over poles from tree limbs to make temporary dwellings. Little children played with a few sticks and a toy. A mother, looking forlorn, sat in the doorway of one makeshift tent while a few others poked at smoldering campfires, their smoke drifting over the crude campground. A man tinkered with his Model T Ford.

"That is similar to the Hoovervilles," his father replied, leaning out the window of his Ford Roadster pickup to get a better look. "Those are some of the people who came from back east because of the Dust Bowl in Oklahoma and Texas. I heard say they lost almost everything they owned." He grabbed at his hat, which threatened to fly out the window, and swerved slightly to miss a pothole in the road.

Those people are really poor, Sheldon thought as he examined the campground. At least he had a place to live and food to eat. He recalled that a boy at school had called him a poor Grover. But these people really didn't have much. He wouldn't ever want to lose their house and live in a tent.

"It looks pretty dumpy there," Merven said. "I wonder if it's even legal for them to be here."

A mosquito landed on the dash, and Sheldon swatted at it. Dust puffed up behind the pickup as they rumbled along the dirt road leading up to the bridge. They drove across the bridge and back along the river until they reached the smoldering campfires. The Ford pickup came to a crunching stop and a few children dropped their sticks to stand and stare. The middle-aged man whose legs were sticking out from under the Model T hood crawled out and stood. He rubbed his eyes and looked at the Grovers with wonder.

"Howdy. Can I help you folks?"

"Just wondering if you might need something to do," Walter said with a smile.

"Well, what ya got in mind?" The man squared his shoulders. "It sure would be nice to have a bit 'o income to help put some food on the table. 'Specially with the missus just having a young 'un, it shore would be nice. Just crossed the Tehachapi Pass last month," he added. He twirled the wrench around his finger several times as if counting the dollars he was stuffing into his flat wallet already. A couple of children stepped closer to see what was going on.

"Well, if you want to come along to see where I live, you may follow me," Walter replied, pointing to the man's car. "I've got an orchard and dry yard with work waiting for you."

"No problem, sir," answered the man. "My name's Harry, by the way. I'll be right along. Let me tell the missus where I be goin' and I'll get my car cranked up." Harry walked away, the little children tagging along behind him to see him off. Smoke drifted across the grounds. The forlorn woman stared out across the river, and then turned and watched him leave. A slight breeze wafted the smoke among the tops of the tall trees.

"Pop," Merven asked, pointing behind them, "do you think we can trust them to work for us in the orchards?" The boys watched the two heads bobbing in the car trailing them. Harry had found a companion, a boy whom

Harry introduced as Jeb. He looked about fifteen years old and had agreed to ride along to see the Grover orchard.

"Well," Walter said, pushing back his hat, "I think they will work hard since they really need money. This also will give us an opportunity to help them as they help us. The Scripture says, 'As we have therefore opportunity, let us do good unto all men.'[1] We may even be able to ask them to go with us to our Sunday meetings sometime if we treat them with respect. Many people treat these families from the Dust Bowl unkindly and look down on them just because they're poor."

After a twenty-minute drive, they reached home. The pickup bumped across the wooden canal bridge and into their dry yard where the fruit would soon be laid out to dry, the sputtering car close behind. The pickup stopped abruptly and dust rolled up from the underside; the Model T came to a halt dangerously close to the pickup. The car was still rocking as the passengers jumped out, anticipating the discussion ahead.

"Here is the peach orchard," Walter said with a sweep of his hand. "We could use help gathering the peaches, swamping the boxes, and then cutting and drying the fruit. If you know any women or girls who would like to cut peaches, that also would be great."

"Not a problem, not a problem. We will be most happy to help." Harry craned his neck to look around at the orchards. "Nice farm," he said as he rubbed his dark beard.

"Thank you. So it's a deal then," said Walter, shaking Harry's hand. "We will see you and Jeb back here on Monday morning at seven o'clock."

A normal weekend passed and soon Monday rolled around. The morning broke clear and bright with people getting out for another week of work.

"Be sure to feed the rabbits, Sheldon," Merven reminded him. "I already gave them water, but I need to do the milking." It was chore time. A couple of hens squawked out of the way as Sheldon grabbed the feed scoop. The work horses whinnied and banged in their stalls.

---

[1] Galatians 6:10

Sheldon enjoyed the cool mornings in the barn. This was the outdoors. This is what he liked best—except for the chickens. He could do without them. If only there would be another way to produce eggs. Hearing a rooster crow in the early mornings was okay with him, but the hens flapping their wings just stirred up too much dust. He sneezed just thinking about it.

"Look, here come Harry and Jeb," Sheldon informed Merven, pointing to the lane. Merven rose from his milking stool to look out through the barn door. Harry's Model T rattled across the canal bridge and into the dry yard.

"And there goes Pop," Merven said. The boys heard the kitchen door slam and boots rustle over sandy soil.

The boys continued their chores amid the sounds of milk swishing into pails and grain tinkling into trays for the rabbits. The smell of alfalfa hay permeated the air and sunlight peeked through the barn boards, throwing slivers of light.

"I'm finished. I'm heading in," Sheldon said.

"And the milking is done," Merven said as he stood and stretched. "There comes Pop."

"What are your plans today?" Ida asked at the breakfast table.

"I have a couple of hired hands out loading the boxes to take to the orchard for picking," Walter replied. "We need to head out and get a load of fruit into the cutting shed so the women and young 'uns can begin cutting and laying them out on the drying trays. Grandpa Ira will probably be out soon too."

The morning passed swiftly as Sheldon helped wherever he was needed. The peaches were picked, put into the wooden boxes, and set along the lanes in the orchard. Then in a process known as swamping, the workers loaded the boxes onto horse-drawn wagons to be transported from the orchard to the cutting shed. The women and children worked swiftly, cutting the peaches in half and laying the fruit on the drying trays. Next, the trays were loaded onto a makeshift railcar and pushed to the sulfur shed where the peaches were treated overnight to maintain their color. Then they were removed and laid out under the California sun to dry.

"Shel-*don!* Chase that cow away!" The shout came from the work area.

Sheila, one of the migrant workers, pointed to a cow ambling toward the dry yard. No one wanted all the hard work of drying peaches to be ruined under the hooves of an ignorant cow.

"Ho!" Sheldon shouted as he ran to head off the animal, but the stubborn creature kicked up her heels and tore across the dry yard, crushing fruit trays as she ran. A dried peach flew through the air. The cow ran off, bucking through the orchard and out of sight. A scrub jay strained his neck, screamed harshly, and flew up to another branch to watch the galloping creature below. The cow's hungry bellow ended on a high note as she disappeared.

Whose cow was that? wondered Sheldon as he began to make order of the trays that had been trampled. Some of the peaches had to be pitched, but most were still salvageable. *Maybe some owner couldn't afford to feed the animal anymore and just turned it loose,* Sheldon thought as he trudged back to the cutting shed.

The day passed quickly as the Grovers and their helpers worked hard to harvest and cut the peaches for drying. Conversations focused on local news, the hope for a better economy, or sometimes just friendly banter. After a long day of work in the sunshine and dust, everyone was always ready to wash up, eat, and call it another day in the San Joaquin Valley.

Sometimes Ida would send Sheldon to the canal to catch a few fish for supper if they hadn't had meat for a while. He didn't have to go far, as the canal cut through their property.

"Do you think you could catch a few fish for supper, Sheldon?" Mama would ask.

"Yippee, I love to fish!" he exclaimed.

"Good, we need some meat."

Finding a nice spot beside the canal, Sheldon baited a fierce-looking Mustad hook and swung it out into the water. Sometimes the fish didn't bite, or perhaps they were simply not in that part of the canal. On this particular evening, Trixie, the family dog, lay beside Sheldon and waited. Her ears perked and she watched intently when a gopher popped out to examine them for a moment before it darted away.

After an hour of relaxing beside the canal and catching a couple of good-sized fish, Sheldon wrapped up his fishing line and threw the remaining earthworms into the canal. "This will have to do for today," he told Trixie as they walked home. "It isn't much, but it's better than no meat at all." Trixie barked as if to say, "That's okay."

"Where were you?" Merven asked gruffly as he spotted Sheldon trudging up. He was sitting on a piece of wood next to the shop.

Sheldon held up his bucket. "Mama wanted me to see if I could catch some fish. By the way, what do you have there?"

"A barrel," answered Merven. "What did you think it was?"

"I meant, what are you going to do with it?"

"That's actually something I was going to ask you to help me with," said Merven. "Take the fish to Mama and come help me." Sheldon quickly put his fishing pole up into the shop rafters and took the bucket of fish to the kitchen.

"Mama," he said. "Merven wants me to help him."

"Okay," agreed his mom. "But don't go too far away because we need to eat after I fry the fish." The kitchen door banged as Sheldon ran out.

"So what are we making?" Sheldon asked, his hands propped on his hips.

"A newfangled shower," Merven said matter-of-factly.

"A shower?" Sheldon was dubious.

"Yes, a shower. Ever hear of one?"

"Why, yes, I've read about them somewhere," answered Sheldon. "Water squirts out of a pipe above you somehow. Are we going to pivot this barrel and have thirty gallons of water gush onto us all at once? We'll drown if we're looking up."

"Are you laughing at my idea?" Merven asked indignantly. "No, we'll attach a pipe with a shut-off valve on it, and we'll also design a head on the pipe with holes in it. Then we'll put it up on a stand and make three sides and a curtain for a door. And presto, a newfangled shower. No more trying to cram ourselves into a large metal basin like poor folks. What do you think?"

"I want to try it out!" said Sheldon.

"Well, we have to get it built first."

"Your wish is my command as long as I have showering rights." Sheldon grinned at Merven. His brother was smart about some things. Now if they could just get this thing to work.

Like many of their friends, the Grovers learned to either make do or figure out a way to overcome a hardship or setback. It wasn't always bad to lack resources or improvise. The old saying was still true, necessity is the mother of invention. Either they learned to be content without something or they made their own.

However, a major setback was about to visit the community that not even the wise or the well prepared could anticipate. Though it was a trial that would severely test their patience, they did not let it get them down.

But for now, at the end of a pleasantly normal day, Ida was looking forward to serving her family the evening meal. "Suppertime!" she called.

chapter three
GOD'S WAY IS PERFECT

1932–1937

Darkness blanketed Modesto as the two figures darted from tree to tree and crossed a meadow. Flames broke through the wall of the building and threw light into the surrounding fields. Soon the people of the neighborhood and the larger community would be streaming in to watch the burning. Silently the two mysterious men observed the arriving fire department and people from the surrounding area.

"Boys! Wake up. There's a fire on Dakota Avenue!"

"Get up, Merven!" Ten-year-old Sheldon shook his older brother. "Pop says there is a fire somewhere on Dakota Avenue."

"What? A fire. Who cares . . . I want to sleep."

"Come on," Sheldon yanked on his trousers and shirt. "Let's go see what's happening."

"Another short night," groaned Merven as he groped for his clothes.

"You'd better hurry because Pop's not going to wait on you," called Sheldon as he rushed out of the bedroom. Walter was already dressed and putting on his boots. He stood up and grabbed his sweater.

"Get your jacket, son. Is Merven coming?"

"I think he is," replied Sheldon, yanking on his boots and grabbing his light jacket. They stepped out into the cool night air. Cars and trucks were rumbling by as more neighbors headed toward the orange glow in the north. The Grovers' Ford pickup sputtered and rumbled to life. Merven jumped in and slammed the door and the tires spun into reverse. Soon they too were following the traffic on Dakota Avenue.

"Pop, that's not a house fire, that's our church house!" gasped Sheldon, wide-eyed. "What happened?"

"I don't know, son." Walter pulled up behind a Model T car and shut off the pickup. "There's Brother Jake. Let's go see what he says."

"We're really not sure what happened," Jake Cover answered soberly. As one of their ministers, Jake, as well as his wife Mary, was respected and loved by many in the church and community. "It could have been arson or it could have been electrical. The fire chief and a few men will be investigating the cause, but really, who will ever know?"

The last section of a wall and a remaining corner collapsed, sending up a shower of sparks into the clear night air. There was a gasp from the men and women along the street and tears streamed down many a face. The beloved Wood Colony Meetinghouse was history. Tears fell as they recalled the many souls that had been saved through sound preaching, the Love Feasts, the grieving times of saying goodbye to a loved one, and the many other good times they had had in this building. It wasn't just another building; it was their life. The structure had been built in 1911 and enlarged twice to hold the hundreds of people who worshiped there.

The fire still devoured the piles of fallen timbers while nearby tree branches and leaves waved in the wind of the flames. Neighbors, church members, and friends stood arm in arm looking on helplessly as the fire crackled and snapped. How would they rebuild? And where would the funds come from to build another church when money already didn't reach around? Was this the hand of God as a result of all the troubles within the congregation this past year? Thoughts like sparks flashed continually as the fire began to slowly die down.

As dawn began to erase the night, the chalky smell of ashes settled over the surrounding landscape. People slowly turned to leave and vehicles sputtered and coughed to life. Small groups of bystanders began to drift homeward as light filtered through the trees along the quiet morning streets.

The Grovers also drove home and a few minutes later the pickup came to a stop beside the house. The doors swung open on the Ford pickup as Walter and the boys got out.

"Even the birds are quiet this morning," remarked Sheldon. "Could nature know what happened too?" The pickup door closed behind him with a clunk.

Merven elbowed him in the ribs. "You need more sleep. I for one am going to hit the sack the first chance I get." He glanced at Pop to gauge his mood.

"Time to do the chores now, boys," said Walter heavily as they filed into the kitchen. He hung his coat on the hook beside the door. "Let's get something to drink and then head out to the barn."

Sheldon kicked off his boots and hung his jacket on the hook below his name.

/ /

"Pop, when are we going to rebuild our church house?" Vera asked as she glanced out the car window. They were driving along Dakota Avenue.

"There is talk of starting next spring." Walter slowed the car as they passed the site of the previous church building. All that was left was a clean lot, a few lonely trees, and a graveyard.

I wonder why God allowed that to happen if He is all-powerful, mused Sheldon as he smoothed back his wind-ruffled hair and rolled the window up a notch. He picked a bit of straw off his Sunday pants. *He could have kept our Wood Colony church house from burning if He had wanted to.* Sheldon's busy mind worked on the problem of evil despite God's sovereignty.

Soon the Grovers' Chevy was parked alongside a few other vehicles around

Maple Hall in Salida, a town that lay next to Modesto. Maple Hall was now used for services and special occasions since the church had burned. The Wood Colony Hall in Modesto was also used frequently, when it was available. Altogether, they would spend four years having services in community buildings or simply visiting other churches. By then, the folks at Wood Colony were more than ready to have a meetinghouse of their own again.

On this particular Sunday morning, the Grovers were, as was normal, among the first to arrive for services. There was no need to hurry as they left their vehicle and walked toward Maple Hall. The acrid smell of crushed walnuts mingled with odors of fermenting apples and just a touch of Baby's Breath lingering on the morning breeze—it was enough to draw a person's mind heavenward. A sparrow twittered and hopped on one of the shrubs next to the hall. Sunlight shimmered over the landscape.

I wonder who will be preaching today? thought Sheldon. *I hope it will be Brother Jake.* He followed his parents into the building. Sitting with his father, he glanced over his shoulder and noticed that his friend Howard Flory was there. The Flory family was also usually among the early arrivals.

The Sunday morning service began as usual, with prayer and a couple of hymns. The congregation's ministers and deacons surrounded a table at the front of the room. The ministers and elders sat facing the room while the deacons sat on the audience side of the table. A pitcher of water and a few cups stood in the center of the table.

Sheldon sat straight and listened intently to the Word of God. He drank in the beauty of holiness that pervaded the atmosphere and thought deeply about the hymns and their poetic meaning. He always looked forward to Sunday morning services and to any solemn occasion such as this.

"Today my sermon will be taken from a thought found in Psalm 18:30," said Charles B. Rumble as he rose to speak. "I will read the verse. 'As for God, his way is perfect: the word of the LORD is tried: he is a buckler to all those that trust in him.' "

As Sheldon listened to the message, he thought about his own life and God's will for him. He wondered what plans God might have in store for him.

"As for God, He is not only perfect Himself, but His way is also perfect," Charles continued. "And as Matthew Henry writes, if God can make the Psalmist's way perfect, He can certainly make His own way perfect."

So the church house burning was not a flaw in the works of God, Sheldon mused.

After the service the brothers and sisters of the Old German Baptist Brethren congregation spent time visiting together. The youth and children also stood in groups and chatted about minor matters.

"So, Sheldon," grinned Howard as he stuck his thumbs in his belt loops, "did you get your aircraft designed yet? The one you plan to fly over to my place? I'd say that's a pretty big job for a skinny fifteen-year-old."

Sheldon's blue eyes twinkled and he squared his shoulders. "What about you and that harvester you've been dreaming about? Did you get it fabricated and into the field?"

A couple other boys drifted over to listen.

"I've been tinkering around with some old parts, but Daddy has me working pretty hard in the harvest, so what can I do? I don't have much time. Maybe when I get older I will show you."

"You fellows think you are inventors, or what?" chuckled Ray Kinzie. His voice lowered. "I'd rather talk about girls."

"Girls," snorted Stanley Filbrun. "Not me. I'd rather go camping in the mountains than deal with them. By the way, Sheldon, do you want to plan a trip to Yosemite sometime?"

"Wow! Now you're onto something. I'd need to talk to Pop to see when it would suit best," said Sheldon. He could already see himself hiking under the majestic giant Sequoias—the largest trees in the world—scaling Half Dome, basking in the mist of Yosemite Falls, or standing on Glacier Point. And then to stop and allow the bitter feeling of the past—the massacred indigenous people groups whose domain this really had been—to overwhelm him. He could hardly wait.

/ /

"Ow!" Sheldon stood rubbing his thumb after he had accidentally hit it while driving a nail.

"Say, how's it going today, Sheldon?" Ray chuckled. "You seeing in a straight line? Or are you looking somewhere else, like . . . maybe the lunch table?"

Sheldon was nailing trusses together with a few other men and boys. He enjoyed swinging a hammer although that wasn't really his area of expertise. Some workers could put a nail in straight every time and not miss a beat, but he would rather be doing something more active any day.

"I am doing my best to do a good job. Not as skilled as some." Sheldon grinned wryly. "At least I am building the church and not tearing it down," he quipped. It felt good to be working on the new church building.

Ever since the Wood Colony Church had burned over on Dakota Avenue, they had been meeting at Maple Hall or Wood Colony Hall. Now they were finally able to work on a new church house—in fact, two new church houses, since they had decided to form two districts. The Modesto District, which Sheldon's family was a part of, had purchased land along Walnut Avenue. They planned to have their first Love Feast and Communion service when the church building was finished. The deadline was November.

"Whew," sighed Stanley Filbrun. "I sure am happy the concrete has been poured for the basement walls. That was hard, dirty work hauling all that gravel and cement and then mixing it by hand. Just the thought of it makes me sweat." He wiped his forehead.

"Aw, it wasn't that bad," retorted Merven. "It helps keep you fit when you work hard. You could use a few extra muscles anyhow, right?"

"Maybe brain muscles," grinned Ray shrewdly, but Stanley didn't comment further.

Soon the trusses were finished and stacked in preparation for installation. A group of men and boys had the walls raised and braced. Others worked in the basement area, and still others were framing interior walls and partitions of the first floor.

"Lunch time!" Jake called. As the men and boys gathered around, he observed, "It is a blessing and an encouragement when we can all work together for a common goal. These work days and times together here remind me of the words in Nehemiah, 'So built we the wall; and all the wall was joined together unto the half thereof: for the people had a mind to work.' "[1]

After the blessing on the noon meal, men and boys washed their hands at a basin of water and stepped to the food line without being told. After the hard work of the morning, the smell of ham sandwiches was inviting.

"My mouth is watering and my stomach hollering for food," said Stanley as he stepped in front of Ray.

"Hey you! Where are your manners?" Ray gave Stanley a good-natured jab with his thumb.

"I hung them on your peg of mischief," Stanley retorted. He helped himself to two ham sandwiches and a couple of deviled eggs. "Come on, Sheldon. Hurry up, I'm hungry."

"You are welcome to go around me if you wish," replied Sheldon. He chose a cup of sweet tea and stepped out of the way. Women and girls laid out more food as trays were emptied. Potluck dinners were always fun times. Good food and friends, and as often as not it was out in the California open air.

"Would you like dessert?" asked Flossie Rumble, a minister's wife. "Maybe a cookie or a piece of pie to take with you?" She motioned in the direction of the desserts. Sheldon glanced at the sweets and then back at Flossie and her daughter beside her. The tart smell of cherries drew his attention. He grinned and shrugged his shoulders shyly.

After much hard labor and many workdays, the Modesto District church house was finished. And the day had finally come for the first Love Feast for the new district and new church house. There was much excitement in the air as the people started to arrive. It had taken five years from cleaning up ashes to this special day.

The Grovers pulled into the parking lot on the west side of the new church building and parked next to a Studebaker. Vehicles in various degrees of repair

---

[1] Nehemiah 4:6

carved fresh tracks into the neatly-raked gravel as they parked.

"Watch it," said Walter as a Model T pulled in beside them. "Had one of you opened a door just then, he would have taken it off. They must be in a hurry, the way he pulled in here."

Walter and Ida strolled to the church house with Vera and Sheldon following right behind. The church parking lot was humming with activity. As cars pulled into parking positions, engines sputtered to silence. Families greeted families. Car doors slammed. Children smiled and waved to each other. The newly planted Modesto Ash trees swayed slightly as they resisted the northwestern breeze. The tule fog—a thick ground fog common to the area—had lifted and water droplets on the trees sparkled in the sunshine.

The Saturday morning service began at 10 a.m. with prayer and a few lined hymns. Afterward a minister preached from Isaiah 53, as was traditional. He spoke about the fulfilled prophecy of the Messiah's coming and God's satisfaction at the suffering and death of His Son for sin.

The inspirational message was followed by a dinner of boiled beef with bread and broth soup, pickles, canned peaches, and applesauce. Members, children, and visitors ate the noon meal together.

At 2 p.m. the group met for another hour of worship, after which families took visitors home to relax, rest, and refreshen before heading back to the church house for the evening service. The Love Feast celebration was an all-day affair, much anticipated and thoroughly delightful.

Sheldon enjoyed the day with his friends but was thinking deeply about his own life. He knew that he was not ready to meet his Maker, yet he wanted to be prepared. He also wanted to experience what he was witnessing today. How long should he wait before he made that commitment? *What if the Lord would return?*

chapter four
A THANKSGIVING CEREMONY

1937

Sheldon picked up another branch and pitched it onto the small brush pile he had started. A skinny rabbit shot out and bounded away. It momentarily stopped to look back before it hopped beyond Sheldon's sight through the orchard. It was a beautiful autumn morning with the sun straining to peer through the tule fog and birds twittering throughout the orchard. He sighed and breathed deeply. Memories of the weekend would not leave him alone as he worked steadily cleaning the orchard. *What did Joel Bowman preach yesterday about the Second Coming of Christ? It could be at any time.* "Imminent" was the word he had used; it meant impending or about to happen. Sheldon had looked it up when he got home from the service to find the exact definition.

Sheldon shuddered to think about the accident the Murrays had had two years ago. It had been a Christmas afternoon, and Robert, who was fifteen at the time, was riding along with his uncle John Murray on a motorcycle.

Near their home in Salida, they hit an electric pole. John, aged 30, was killed instantly, and Robert died the next morning. Neither had been baptized or a part of the church. *Imminent. Death could also happen at any time.*

A heavy weight settled over Sheldon as he worked. The joy of working outdoors and especially in the orchard was pushed aside by something much more pressing.

"What's the matter with you, son?" asked Walter gruffly as he brought the horse and rake through the orchard between the peach trees. The rake was used to drag the fruit prunings out of the orchards to a larger pile that would be burned. "Are you sick?"

"Oh, I'll be okay," said Sheldon quickly. At the slap of the reins on her back, Adios moved forward again to rake more of the brush out of the orchard to a growing pile. The sun seemed to stand still as Sheldon forked branches and twigs into the path between the trees. A light breeze carried the smell of smoke through the orchard. Grandpa had met them in the morning and said he planned to start burning some of the brush and branches. He said he would also spend some time pruning grapevines.

I have disobeyed Pop and Mama behind their backs, Sheldon thought. *I have sinful thoughts at times that I know are wrong. Maybe I am not good enough for God.*

Adios shook her harness as she came to a stop and stood for a moment. She lowered her head to find a tuft of grass to nibble. Walter let the reins slide through his hands. Sheldon paused for a moment to glance at Pop who had reined in the horse.

"I am going to take Adios back to the barn now and check on Grandpa and the fire," Pop said in a business-like manner. "Keep doing what you're doing." With that he slapped the reins and was off again, dragging more branches.

Imminent. Impending or about to happen. The words kept coming back to Sheldon as he worked. *God, I want to be prepared.*

Then the still small voice . . . *You can be prepared. Behold, I stand at the door, and knock: if any man hear my voice, and open the door, I will come in to him, and will sup with him, and he with me. To him that overcometh will I grant to sit with me in my throne.*[1] *I didn't come to save good people. I came to save sinners . . .* God's Spirit whispered gently but persistently.

Looking around, Sheldon knelt beside a large peach tree and whispered a prayer as a tear slid down his cheek. "God, I want to be prepared for the Second Coming. I want to serve you. I don't want to perish. I want to have everlasting life."

The heavy burden lifted as Sheldon stood and looked around at the orchard. The peach trees seemed to dance and clap in the breeze and suddenly birds twittered thither and yon. A ray of sunlight fell on his face. *Is God here?* It was so real. A wide grin split his face. *I'll find a way to tell Pop tonight. He'll want to call Brother Charles Rumble in plenty of time before our next church service.* Sheldon burst into a song of praise as he worked.

/ /

The brush fire in the orchard had burned down by evening, leaving a bed of hot coals. Around the fire sat the Grovers as they roasted wiener sausages and enjoyed the evening stillness. Some of the family sat on crates. Others sat on pieces of wood. In the distance, a hound howled. Red-hot coals glistened in the darkness and a few sticks of wood were added to flare up some light. Grandpa Ira poked the smoldering pieces of peach wood with a long stick.

"So what do you think will happen with the feud between the Pacific Gas & Electric Company and the Modesto Irrigation District?" Ira asked as he pushed a smoldering chunk of wood up onto another. "Think they'll settle on something?"

"Don't know. It's been fifteen or more years, hasn't it?" replied Walter.

"Too long. You'd think as frequently as Modesto Irrigation District has cut power rates the last five years, Pacific Gas & Electric would give up and sell."

"I think I see the handwriting on the wall," said Walter as he wrapped another wiener in bread. "It can't go on forever."

"It sure is nice having indoor lighting," added Maggie. She passed a bowl

---
[1] Revelation 3:20-21

of sliced tomatoes around the circle. "It seems only a few years ago that we carried lanterns and used candles."

"They put in utility poles when Sheldon was just a baby, so it's been about fourteen years," replied Ida, turning the stick in her hand as she roasted another wiener.

Now this is real living, mused Sheldon. *Even if we don't have a lot of money.* He savored the simple foods and the cool evening air.

Vera sat cross-legged on the loamy California soil, unconcerned about her clothes getting wrinkled or dusty. *The only thing my sisters have in common,* Sheldon thought, *is their last name.* He liked his sisters but he did miss Merven. Merven was now married to Pauline Filbrun and lived over on the Flory farm in a one-room cabin. It was too bad they didn't live closer. His sister Frieda had married Delmer Denlinger and they had moved back east, all the way to Ohio.

The fire had died down along with the conversation and the ladies began to gather up the utensils and food and take them to the house. Ira, Walter, and Sheldon remained by the dying embers. Hundreds of bull frogs croaked in the nearby canal and splashed into the water as the ladies walked past them. Crickets joined the chorus and a mockingbird sang close by. Nervously, Sheldon cleared his throat. *There will never be a better time than this,* he decided.

"Pop," he said quietly. "I would like to be baptized." He could see the outline of his father and grandpa against the night sky. Stars were twinkling in the heavens and the moon was beginning to rise as he waited, heart pounding.

"Well," said his father heartily, "I am glad to hear this, son. Are you ready to commit your life to Jesus and obey the church?" Walter peered intently at his son from under bushy brows.

"Yes, Pop," said Sheldon as he stood quietly thinking about his encounter with God in the orchard. His heart leapt with joy as he thought of baptism and the privilege of being a part of God's kingdom.

"Very well," Walter looked at Ira, who was listening in on his grandson's request. "We should contact Brother Charles, shouldn't we?"

"Yes," nodded Ira approvingly. He clapped Sheldon's shoulder with his strong hand as the three headed for the house.

/ /

"I think I hear a car pulling up," said Vera, staring out the window. "It looks like Charles' car." She sat down again on the chair and smoothed out her dress. A few moments later, there was a light knock on the door.

"Come in," Walter's voice boomed as he opened the door wide and beckoned.

"Good evening, Brother Walter and Sister Ida." Elder Charles B. Rumble and Minister Jake Cover shook hands with the Grover family. For a moment, Ida's memory flashed back to that Christmas night when Jake's wife Mary came to help with Sheldon's birth. *Another prayer answered,* Ida thought.

"Make yourselves at home," said Ida warmly, "and find yourselves comfortable chairs."

"And now, Sheldon." Charles and Jake turned their attention to him, after they had made a bit of small talk. "We are glad to hear of your choice to follow the Lord. And we understand you wish to be baptized and become a part of the church. Is this correct?" Sheldon had taken care to be dressed well and had combed his hair neatly. He was excited and yet nervous about the interview.

"Yes. I want to be baptized," replied Sheldon quietly.

"We would like to go over a few principles this evening to make sure you are able and willing to count the cost of following the Lord," began Charles. His face was sober.

"The three primary points of discussion will be non-resistance or non-retaliation, non-conformity, and the non-swearing of oaths." Charles turned to related passages of Scripture to read and explain the simple and yet profound truths of God's Word. Sheldon listened intently. *Will I be able to deny self, take up my cross and follow Jesus?* He pondered the clear teachings of Jesus. *It would be better not to vow, than to vow and not pay.*[2] *Yes, it is still*

---

[2] Ecclesiastes 5:5

what I want to do.

Brother Charles continued. "It is very important to carefully fill your mind with the Word of God and to meditate upon His precepts. The Proverbs writer says, 'Keep thy heart with all diligence; for out of it are the issues of life.'[3] The Bible also says, 'Thy word have I hid in my heart, that I might not sin against thee.'[4] It is important to spend time in prayer to maintain a close and vibrant walk with the Lord."

After carefully explaining the principles the Brethren held as vital to the Christian life, the minister asked Sheldon if he understood and was willing to uphold each one. The family then knelt for prayer with the ministers at the end of the instruction time.

"We normally leave the date of baptism open to the individuals. Is there a certain day you would like to be baptized, Sheldon?" Charles asked. "We are planning a baptism for this Thursday, Thanksgiving Day, if you would like to join the group."

"This Thursday would be okay with me," said Sheldon. His heart thumped uncomfortably as he thought about standing in front of the whole church to confirm his commitment to Christ. He squirmed a bit in his chair. He never did like being the focus of attention, but at least his part wouldn't last too long. After his parents and sisters had gone to bed, Sheldon remained beside the stove and listened to the fire spit and snap. The blue gum wood he had added to the coals caused the stove to heat quickly. He stretched and leaned back on the chair. Could he be faithful until death? Would he receive the crown of life? He would trust in the keeping power of God and set a goal to remember that Jesus could return at any time. His return was imminent. Impending.

The chiming clock awoke Sheldon from his contemplation, and he sighed and rose to his feet. "I had better get some rest," he said aloud. The door squeaked slightly as he entered his room. He was now looking forward to

---

[3] Proverbs 4:23
[4] Psalm 119:11

Thanksgiving Day for more than one reason.

Wednesday passed slowly for Sheldon as he anticipated the next day's special service. Whether it was chore time, cleaning the vineyards, or carrying wood for his grandparents, his mind was thinking over this important step. *This is the most important choice I will ever make,* he mused. *I want to reign with the Lord Jesus when He returns.*

Thanksgiving Day dawned with a bit of fog that soon vanished with the rising sun. A large breakfast awaited Sheldon when he and Pop came in from feeding the animals. Piles of pancakes and scrambled eggs, stacks of golden brown toast, fried potatoes, and maple syrup were filling the kitchen with wonderful smells. A special meal was okay once in a blue moon, Pop had said, but too often could spoil them.

As soon as breakfast is over, I must shower and dress for the service, Sheldon thought as he cleaned up the last of his potatoes. He wanted to be dressed properly for this important occasion.

"It's time to be going," Walter's gruff voice rang through the house as he strode for the door. "Everyone to the car." A few minutes later, the family's Chevy car rolled out the long lane.

Pop guided the car around potholes or over rough spots in the dirt and gravel streets as they rumbled along. The ride to church didn't seem as long as usual. When they pulled off Walnut Street and into the church parking lot, Sheldon's stomach filled with butterflies. *I will need to stand up in front of every one and speak. Can I do that?* He swallowed hard.

At the end of the yearly Thanksgiving Day service, Elder Charles B. Rumble stood for announcements.

"It has been brought to our attention that a few of our young brethren have requested water baptism. We have interviewed them and their families, and are confident they are ready and able to take this step. We will ask them to stand at this time.

"Gilbert Grover, Weston Bauman, Dale Rumble, Maurice Boyd, and Alvah Sheldon Grover, would you please stand?"

"These applicants for baptism," Charles went on, "have agreed to comply with the questions we asked concerning the doctrines held by the church. They are willing to submit to the church's counsel and disciplines."

Sheldon stood and clenched his Bible close in fingers that trembled slightly. The boys were then asked to publicly acknowledge their need of a Savior. After they had taken turns affirming their desire for baptism, the boys and their immediate family members were dismissed to the basement while one of the ministers walked along the aisles and asked the members if they were willing to accept each applicant as a member.

Sheldon's heart throbbed as he contemplated the approaching ordinance that would symbolize the work of Jesus in his life. He wanted to please God with all his heart, soul, and mind out of his gratitude for what had been done for him. Now he had a living hope! A hope not dependent on social status or on how much money he had. His heart was full.

After the leadership took the voice of the church, a deacon called the families back into the sanctuary. The young men were called to the front of the church to sit directly in front of the Elder who would perform the baptism.

"I will read a passage from Matthew 18 and ask a few questions before we dismiss," the Elder said, choosing the traditional passage of Scripture read at baptisms. After he finished reading, the five boys were asked to acknowledge their understanding and willingness to maintain humble and workable relationships with all members of the church.

"If offenses should arise, are you willing to take the pattern described by our Lord in making reconciliation and peace?"

"I am."

Elder Charles explained, for all who planned to attend, where they would be going for the baptism.

A spot on the Stoddard Ranch along the Stanislaus River had been chosen for the ceremony. Grandpa Ira and his son Jay Grover, both deacons, had walked this area the day before to find a good spot for the riverside service. Uncle Jay had placed a stake in the river where the water was deep and clean.

Vehicles pulled off Stoddard Road and parked at the chosen spot along the bank of the Stanislaus River. A path had been cleared through the brush to allow for easier access to the baptismal site. Sheldon walked down to the river's edge with his friends and family and those who had come for the special occasion.

He removed his only pair of Sunday shoes and placed them carefully on a large protruding boulder on the riverbank. Since he had left his suit coat in the car, he was dressed only in a white cotton shirt and dark grey pants. It was partly sunny and cool with temperatures in the mid-50s. A light northerly wind was sending occasional ripples over the water and causing a few leaves to flutter south. The willow trees whispered in the wind while people waited quietly at the river's edge.

At Charles' request, Sheldon waded out to him and knelt at his side. His shoulders and head remained uncovered as he listened to the questions.

"Do you believe that Jesus is the Son of God and that He brought a saving Gospel?"

"I do."

"Do you renounce Satan and all his pernicious practices and the sinful pleasures of this world?"

"I do."

"Do you covenant with God in Christ Jesus to remain faithful unto death?"

"I do."

"Upon your confession of faith before God and these witnesses, I baptize you in the name of the Father . . ."

Elder Charles leaned Sheldon forward into the water until he was fully submerged and then brought him back up.

"And the Son . . ."

Another plunge forward.

"And the Holy Ghost."

A third time. Water poured off Sheldon's head onto his shoulders as he came up. His face radiated the inner warmth and peace of the new birth experience.

Charles then placed his hands upon Sheldon's head. He prayed that Sheldon's sins would be forgiven, that his name would be written in the

Lamb's Book of Life, and that he would receive the gift of the Holy Spirit.

After the Christian salutation of a holy kiss, Charles said, "The Lord bless and keep you."

Wading out of the river, Sheldon shivered from the cold, but his heart was throbbing with warmth. A towel was quickly handed to him to dry up the dripping water. He wiped his face and head and patted his clothing. His mother Ida handed him a warm heavy coat. After donning the coat, he sat on the protruding rock to put on his shoes, and then quietly stood beside the river to watch the baptism of the other youth. All of them would then be greeted and welcomed into the church by the brothers and sisters before returning to their homes.

Sheldon stood soberly on the sandy bank. He sensed God's presence and approval. He was at peace. Now he belonged to a brotherhood, a church family. What all did the Lord have in store for him? What experiences would involve the cross-bearing and self-denial the ministers spoke about? Only time could tell.

chapter five
HALF DOME OR BUST

1941

Six boys, all in their late teens, had left early in the morning for a trip to Yosemite National Park and were thoroughly enjoying themselves.

"Keep your eyes on the road, Pop," Donald said to Sheldon, who was driving. "We don't need to slide this shiny black Chevy over the side and crash."

"Don't worry, Mom," Sheldon tossed the comment to his sidekick. "I'll do the best I can. After all, we have four kids in the back."

"We're not kids. We're associate travelers."

Sheldon grinned to himself as he skillfully guided his 1936 Chevy around another bend in the road. Look at him now. He had bought this shiny black Chevy sedan that was only a couple of years old and in mint condition. He had a good job in orchard keeping and was able to do some research on how to improve his skills with growing trees and plants. Now if he could just find the right girl, he could erase some more of the stigma he felt because of how poor he was. He knew it wasn't wrong to be poor, but somehow he always felt that shame associated with having too little. Or maybe it was just their culture dictating these feelings.

Sheldon slowed the car a bit to pass a fallen boulder. "Donald, can you see how close we are to the edge? See, I'm taking your comment seriously. No need for us to die somewhere on the side of this mountain," said Sheldon as he steered around the large boulder.

The sun was glinting over the Sierras as they neared Crane Flat. It was a clear July morning and soon the sun's rays would be scorching.

"Shall we pull in and get some gas?" Sheldon asked, pointing ahead. He throttled back and braked as they bumped toward the Crane Flat gas station. "I think we had better fill up."

"Not a problem with me," said Stanley. "I would rather stop and get some 'Gassy Wassy' than run out somewhere back in these hills."

"I think it's a good time to go chase a few rabbits too," said Gerald as he got out and stretched. "It hasn't been that long since we left home, but all that bouncing has me needing to find a grove of trees where rabbits run."

"Just come back in one piece, Jerry," chortled Allen. "We don't need you coming back with souvenir bear bites."

Before long, the Chevy was purring along the high mountain roads once more, kicking up a wake of fine dust. By now, the shiny black car had a sheen of brown powder over it and dust shimmied on the bumpers.

"Did your headlights meet your taillights on that last switchback, Pop?" asked Sam as he let out a long breath. "Some of these switchbacks are just plain crazy. I think it would be better to take the new road next time."

"Something is rumbling somewhere," Sheldon's voice tensed. "Do you hear it?" He slowed the Chevy to a stop and switched off the engine. The distant rumble now seemed closer and the roar grew louder. The boys peered out the windows to see behind them. To their dismay a rock and land slide tumbled onto a portion of the road they had just traveled.

"Whew, that was close," said Sheldon shakily as he started the engine and let out the brake.

"Far too close for comfort," Stanley was more emphatic. "Maybe the vibrations from the car started the falling rocks. Let's get to Glacier Point."

/ /

"Now this is tremendous!" Sheldon surveyed the valley below and studied the mountain's majestic form. He lowered his binoculars and picked up his camera for another shot of the mighty Half Dome formation with its sheer, flat side.

After arriving, the boys had unloaded their gear and hiked out to Glacier Point's jutting rock where they were enjoying the scenery.

"I heard that Yosemite Falls is one of the world's tallest," commented Sam, pointing to the distant waterfalls to their left. "Does anyone know what the drop is?"

"About twenty-four hundred feet," replied Sheldon. "It's actually comprised of three different levels. We should be able to see it better from the Four-Mile Trail after we climb down to the South Side road."

"Is someone going to do a handstand out on the point?" dared Stanley. "I heard someone actually drove a car out to the edge once."

"They had to be crazy, too," retorted Sam. "I'm not going out to the edge." He backed away with his eyebrows contorted.

"It's been done before." Sheldon put his camera and binoculars beside his backpack. "And if it's been done before, it can be done again. Hey, it's only 3,214 feet down to Curry Village." Walking out to the jutting rock, he flipped down onto his hands and swung his legs up and balanced himself. He would prove himself to be a man among men, he thought.

An unexpected gust of wind sent a chill from his finger tips to the ends of his toes as he wobbled precariously. He dropped back down onto his feet and walked back from the jutting rock ledge, his heart pounding.

"Whew! I was sweating just watching you," Stanley breathed. "I didn't think you'd do it."

"We need to get onto the trail if we want to make it to the Little Yosemite Valley before dark," reminded Donald. "We've got miles to go before we sleep," he quipped.

The hike from Glacier Point down to the main road leading into Yosemite Valley was a delightful beginning to the day. The famous Yosemite Falls could be seen to the north as they walked along the south side of the Merced River. Back along the mountain on the valley floor, they hiked beneath the point on which they had stood a few hours earlier. Sheer granite walls, natural and man-made stone stairways, trails through the coniferous forests, lush green meadows, a wildflower paradise, bounding forest creatures, winging native birds, and much more declared the glory of their Creator.

"Is that a golden eagle up there?" Allen pointed as he stopped momentarily. Far above them circled a giant bird.

"It sure looks like it," said Sam as he raised his binoculars. "They are beautiful birds."

"Gramps was telling me that those big birds will fight with a fox over a kill," added Jerald. "And they'll even attack a young deer when they're ravenous."

"That reminds me," said Donald. "I am very hungry."

"Not a very nice place to spread our lunch." Sheldon looked around. "I guess we can just sit on these rocks. Unless you want to walk till we find a nice grassy spot somewhere."

"I can sit on rocks. I'm starving."

After a light lunch, the hikers were off again. With a five-minute break and a bite to eat, they were refreshed and reenergized.

"Ready to get wet, boys?" asked Stanley as they approached Vernal Falls. The more they continued following Mist Trail up to the falls, the more they could begin to feel the mist. The stone steps were slippery, so they picked their way cautiously. A rainbow rose out of the spraying water. At the top of the climb, the ground leveled and a deceptively calm pool known as Emerald Pool invited them to enjoy its coolness. Water from the pool fed the Vernal Falls and was known to have subtle undercurrents taking waders over the falls to their deaths.

"It feels good to sit down for a bit," remarked Gerald. He lowered himself gingerly onto a large flat rock and wiped his forehead that was wet from a combination of mist and sweat. "How many steps was that?"

"More than 600." Sheldon looked at Gerald with a tight grin. "Getting your exercise?"

"A real workout," Gerald groaned. "You may have to carry me to the top of Half Dome."

The band of six continued to scramble upward through the canyon another thousand feet. They climbed up over granite stone, along moss-covered stone walls, and through dense stands of pine trees. They stopped for a few minutes when they reached the Nevada Falls, but soon they were climbing onward once again.

"Look! I think that's a fisher and her kits," Sheldon pointed through the forest where a shaft of fading sunlight was playing on a stand of Junipers. "Psht. Hold still!" The boys silently watched the Pacific fisher lead her little band through the forest. When the last kit disappeared from sight, Donald spoke.

"Even if that is all we see, our whole trip will have been worth it. That was the first time I saw a mother fisher with a pack of kits."

"She was probably out looking for food, and the young'uns are learning, too," said Stanley. "I think it's time we find our own dinner." The terrain had now changed to a valley floor even though they were at an elevation of around 6,000 feet above sea level.

The sun disappeared behind the mountains, and the shadows lengthened in Little Yosemite Valley as the weary hikers set up camp. Stately firs towered above them, and a stand of Jeffrey pines nearby released a fragrance that smelled like Mama's baking vanilla.

"I'll start gathering wood for a fire," offered Sheldon. "We need to start a fire as soon as possible to cook our meal."

Soon the camp was organized and a fire crackling. The acidic smell of the soup and the charred grill smoke from the meat significantly increased the young men's hunger. If the scale measured between one and ten, their hunger level must have fallen close to eleven.

"Would someone please ask a blessing on this grub so I can eat?" Donald asked as he wrapped a wiener in bread. Six forms were huddled around the fire, their sticks converging over the mounds of coals and flickering flame.

"I'll pray," offered Stanley. After a short prayer, the boys tore into the simple meal of soup and crackers with wieners wrapped in bread.

Work hard, eat well, and sleep deeply, thought Sheldon as he dozed off later.

It was still dark the next morning when the boys awoke. Breakfast consisted of eggs and bacon along with toast fried in the bacon grease. They ate heartily, knowing that the climb to the crest of Half Dome would take plenty of energy.

The valley was still bathed in moonlight as the eager climbers began trekking toward the base of their day's challenge. The ascent from the valley to the base of Half Dome was breezy and cool but not abnormally so. As they hiked higher, the trails changed from gravel and dirt to more stone and granite. The awakening sun touched their faces.

At the base of Half Dome, they began the steep ascent toward the top, using the cables installed for those brave enough to scale the crest of the magnificent granite crown that juts 4,839 feet above the valley floor. With visibility up to ten miles, the view was breathtaking.

"In the beginning, God created," Donald called out above the breeze. "Isn't this gorgeous?"

"When were these cables installed?" Allen asked. "Sure glad they are here."

"They were installed in 1919, which would make it twenty-two years ago," replied Stanley.

The view of the valley below and the surrounding mountains was even more stunning when they finally reached the top. Standing next to the edge of Half Dome's visor, nearly a mile above the Yosemite Valley floor, they silently observed the ingenious artwork of the Designer. The deep Yosemite canyon valley and Sierra Mountain peaks created beautiful contrast.

"It looks a bit dark out over those distant peaks," said Gerald. "Maybe we had better be heading out." Even as he spoke, the boys saw a thin line of light reach out of the clouds to touch the earth many miles away.

"I think that breeze has gotten a bit stiffer, don't you?" asked Donald, turning around. "I am heading down now." As the boys descended Half Dome, the wind kicked up and the skies grew dark. The distant rumbling that had been hardly perceptible was now much nearer.

"Let's get down before the stone becomes slick," hollered Allen. "Those cables are hard to hang on to when they are wet."

The cables slid through their hands, rubbing the skin raw. They were descending as fast as they could while still remaining safe. The danger lay not only in the sheer stone becoming slick because of all the water, but also in the threat of lightning. Their hair began to stand on end from the electricity in the atmosphere. Raindrops began to sting their faces as they neared the base of Half Dome.

Wonder where that storm came from, thought Sheldon as he skidded down the stone surface. *The sky was clear earlier this morning*. He clung to the cable for a moment to catch his breath, then let himself slide again. The boys were making the descent in record time.

For some reason, as Sheldon descended, his thoughts kept going to Mary Ellen Rumble, a young lady from his youth group. He had just begun to notice her at the youth functions and he thought she may have noticed him too. He couldn't be sure, but at least he had plenty of time. She was only seventeen.

Finally, the boys were away from the cables but still a long distance from completely escaping the danger. Rain and wind slashed at their jackets and soaked their gear while the boys slipped and clawed their way down the mountain. Lightning ripped at the skies somewhere farther away. Thunder roared all around them. Forest creatures huddled in thickets. At last, six wet young men trudged into camp exhausted. Thankful. Alive.

/ /

"So how was your trip to Yosemite?"

Sheldon looked up from cleaning his camera. His mother was washing the lunch dishes and had turned her attention to him.

"It was okay. I really enjoyed going with the boys. We went out by way of Big Oak Flat Road, and then came back by the All Year Highway."

"Did you take the newly-constructed Big Oak Road or the old route?" Pop put down the article he was reading and focused his attention on Sheldon.

"We took the old route."

"The road was drivable?" Walter's bushy eyebrows contracted.

"Barely," Sheldon chuckled reminiscently. "A small avalanche took out a portion of the road right behind us at one point."

"Sheldon! No . . ." Ida grimaced and shook her head. "You should have known better than to drive the old route with all those switchbacks and falling rocks."

"All's well that ends well, Mama," said Pop, picking up his paper again.

Sheldon continued to clean his camera and tighten the lens. *I'm glad they don't know how close I came to losing my balance on Glacier Point. No need to worry, Mama. After all, all's well that ends well.*

Sheldon thought about the trip to Half Dome. It had been so enjoyable to be out in nature and climb the dome of that majestic mountain. He loved the outdoors and spent all the time he could working in the fields or orchards, hiking through Yosemite, fishing in the Stanislaus, or photographing nature. One thing was for sure, he would never work in a factory or an office. It just wasn't his nature at all.

chapter six
NO CASUAL DATING

1942–1944

"Sheldon, would you want to go to the singing this evening?" Vera asked. "It will be held at Hubert Rumble's home, and I would like to go."

"Sure, I'd like to go. So I guess that makes two of us." Sheldon stood up from the kitchen table. "What about Pop and Mama? Are they going?"

"Not this evening," said Ida, putting down that month's issue of the German Baptist magazine, *The Vindicator*. "I'll make something light for you all to eat before you go." She rose from her chair, took her apron off its hook, and picked up a half loaf of bread from the breadbox.

After supper, Sheldon and Vera grabbed a couple of songbooks, and headed for the car. They drove along in silence observing the Stanislaus County scenery slide by. When they pulled up to the Rumble home, the springtime sun was hanging low in the western sky and the temperatures were still warm.

"It looks like we will be singing inside the house this evening," said Sheldon. Other youth and families were also walking to the house. Vehicles were parking wherever there was an available spot. Car doors clunked shut. Someone laughed, and a few voices were making small talk. Palm trees and small shrubs hugged the Rumbles' grey brick house. Some California Fuchsia grew next to the porch. The young people entered the house through the screened-in porch. The house door was propped open as if to welcome them in.

"Hey, Pop," Stanley Filbrun mouthed, falling back on the old nickname he used for Sheldon. "Come sit beside me." Vera also found a seat, between Ruth Cover and Mary Ellen Rumble. As more youth and families arrived, the seating was arranged a bit tighter. Some stood to make more room.

The *Brethren Hymnal* was the default songbook at the Old German Baptist singings. Depending on the occasion, they would supplement it with others, such as the *Star of Bethlehem,* the *Gospel Hymns,* or the *Carols of Joy.* Four-part singing was common among their people, and they often gathered to worship in song. Sometimes singings would be held on a weekday evening if there were visitors in the area. In the summertime, singings were often held out on the lawn.

"What do you say, Pop?" asked Stanley. It was after the singing and they were in line to get a few refreshments. Hubert's wife was serving chocolate pieces, fresh cookies, garden tea and coffee.

"What do I say? It's okay to speak if you can improve on silence." Sheldon winked at his friend with his customary tight-lipped smile. "How about you?"

"Let's take a seat over there next to your sister and her friend. That's what I say." He motioned shrewdly to where Vera and Mary Ellen were seated.

"Fine with me," replied Sheldon. He too had noticed the Rumble girl. He grew up knowing almost all these people. Stanley was an exception, since his folks had moved to Modesto five years ago. But somehow he had not really noticed Joseph and Flossie Rumble's daughter until the last year. He had always liked Mary Ellen but somehow she had changed recently. Just the way she carried herself and spoke with the other youth caught his attention. It wasn't a high look but a determined carriage and a lovely disposition.

After getting a handful of goodies and something to drink, the boys navigated their way around the seated men, women, and children.

"Are these seats taken?" asked Stanley as he and Sheldon approached the empty chairs next to the ornate desk and bench where the girls were seated.

"Take your pick," responded Mary Ellen quickly. She turned back to Vera and continued chatting. The voices of adults, youth, and children rose and fell as they fellowshipped.

"So what do you think about the Japanese submarine I-17 that fired those high-explosive shells toward the oil refinery near Santa Barbara?" asked Donald Beachler. He shook his head and took another swallow of coffee.

"I heard it didn't do much damage or maybe none at all," replied Sheldon. "I wonder if the Japanese would actually attack America full swing?"

"I don't know, but I think the United States should stay out of fighting, period," put in Stanley as he popped a piece of chocolate into his mouth. The war was a hot topic because of the potential draft that could affect the young men at a moment's notice. No one knew what the future would hold with war flaring up at hotspots around the world.

There could be a draft, thought Sheldon. *How would that affect a courtship, and would Joseph and Flossie's daughter even be a possibility for me? She is from a well-to-do family and I, well . . . my family could actually be called poor; maybe not as poor as some, but definitely needing to keep our belts tight.* As a boy growing up, he had made or carved his own toys. His family had taken turns bathing on Saturday nights in a large metal tub next to the wood stove. His mind was spinning.

From what he had overheard, some of the local boys were saying that not just anyone could marry a Rumble. Sheldon was sure he could prove himself, but didn't know if he even wanted to bother with pursuing something impossible. But then again, maybe it would be worth the challenge.

A few weeks passed before Sheldon had the opportunity to see Mary Ellen again. He had been sent over to Salida to the C.J. Rumble and Sons packing sheds company on an errand for Pop. Pulling in to the parking area next to the railroad, he jumped out of his car and strode to the offices.

"Come in," someone called from within. Sheldon opened the door and stepped inside. Joseph Rumble was seated at his desk. He smiled as he looked up. Joseph had been elected to the office of minister the same year the new district had been formed and Sheldon had been baptized. Not only was Joseph a good minister but he was also a great entrepreneur.

Joseph's company grew, packed, and shipped watermelons, peaches, cantaloupe, and sweet corn from the packing sheds to places as far away as New York City. Almonds were also hulled and shipped to processing plants.

Sheldon stepped into the spacious office area and looked around. The furniture and décor was up-to-date, the large windows overlooking the railroad were invisibly clear, and a brand spanking new telephone rested on the desktop. A large U.S. map on a windowless wall had small colored pins scattered across it.

"You're probably wondering what the map is about," said Joseph, observing Sheldon's lingering gaze. "Here, let me show you." He stepped out from behind his desk. His boots clicked on the hardwood floor.

"As you can see, most pins cover the Midwest. These are areas where our Dust Bowl migrant workers are from. I wanted to see how consistently the pins touch these selected states—South Dakota, Nebraska, Kansas, Oklahoma, and Texas. There are a few pins in eastern Colorado and New Mexico," he said with a sweep of his hand. "Following years of over-cultivation and poor land management in the 1920s, the region suffered a severe drought in the early 1930s that lasted several years. This area's topsoil was exposed because the native grasses had been removed and the windstorms simply blew the topsoil away or piled it in drifts. Since most of these farmers lost all they had, they came to California to look for work. Now many of these Okies or Dust Bowl migrants work here at our packing sheds."

"Yes sir," replied Sheldon. "We've had a few working for us the last few years too. Merven has hired a few Dust Bowl families to help him with his harvesting and cutting."

"Hard workers, right? But back to you, Sheldon. You must have come for some reason."

"Yes, Pop wanted me to come over and purchase some spray for the fruit trees we should be spraying soon," replied Sheldon. "He thought he might get a better deal from you since you get it in bulk."

"We should have plenty," said Joseph. "We don't have it here, though. You will need to run over to the home place. Get one of the hired hands to help you. Tell them I sent you."

At the Rumble farm on Dale Road, a few farm hands were forking down hay to be fed to the livestock. Someone was out by the roadside stand selling some early vegetables. As Sheldon stepped from his car, he wondered who he should ask for help. He paused momentarily to admire the buildings and grounds. Just then the door to the milk house swung open.

Mary Ellen appeared from the doorway. It seemed every time he saw her, she looked more beautiful than the time before. Sheldon gulped. His hands and feet suddenly felt too big for his body.

"Are you looking for someone?" she asked with a gentle smile.

Sheldon's heart was pounding.

"I was over at the packing sheds talking to your father." Sheldon's voice cracked frustratingly. He cleared his throat. "He said I could come over and get some spray that we need for our trees."

"Let me call Jim for you," said Mary Ellen. "He's in charge around here." She walked out to the barn and called. The skirt of her maroon and grey plaid dress whispered as she walked.

/ /

Sheldon sprayed the dust off his car, using a water hose stretched out from the tank house. Next he grabbed the bucket of soap and water, plunged the rag into the mixture, and carefully washed the car. After thoroughly washing it, he waited for it to dry in the light and mild evening wind. After the car was dry, he opened the can of DuPont Auto Polish and Cleaner and began to clean and polish until the black paint glistened. The sun was just sliding out of sight beyond the Pacific as he finished waxing the prized 1936 Chevy sedan.

As Sheldon cleaned his car, he contemplated his future. During the previous several months, he had been praying for direction. He wanted to be a farmer, to keep orchards and vineyards. That much he knew for sure. And now his thoughts were frequently exploring the idea of asking Mary Ellen that most important question. Marriage—is that what he wanted? He enjoyed his life at home, but knew that eventually he wanted to begin his own family. After all, he didn't want to live his whole life alone. The Bible even said it wasn't good for man to be alone. But even if he was interested in her, that didn't mean she would accept him, a lowly Grover. True to character, Sheldon mulled over his problem in silence as he put away his cleaning supplies.

Some of the youth had planned an all-day trip to Yosemite Park and were meeting the next day at Earl Cover's place to share rides. They were planning a picnic on Glacier Point and anticipating a pleasant day.

The next morning, Sheldon and Vera arrived at the Cover residence a few minutes early.

Sheldon swung out of his car and pushed the door shut behind him. Vera joined her best friend Ruth Cover and other cousins who were peering into backseats and open trunks to make sure they had everything they needed. It wouldn't do to leave something behind. They checked through each basket of food to make sure there would be enough. Somewhere a dog in a backyard raised a ruckus and a flock of domesticated ducks quacked their extreme displeasure. The sun peaked through the tops of the Blue Gum trees and glinted off the car hoods.

"You waxed your Chevy, I see," Don sauntered up to Sheldon who was leaning against his car. Don Beachler was a good friend. "How many coats did you put on it?"

"Enough to keep her good and warm," replied Sheldon with a grin. "You like it?"

"If a bug landed on your car it would slide off and hit the ground."

The youth piled into three vehicles for the trip to Yosemite. Sheldon silently noted that Mary Ellen chose to ride in his car. They were riding six to a car.

"Not you again," teased Sheldon as Stanley squeezed in beside him. He lightly jabbed his elbow into Stanley's ribs. "Why are you riding with me?"

The young people drove along the Merced River on the All Year Highway, enjoying the beauty of a mid-summer morning. California black oaks, ponderosa pines, incense cedars, and white firs blanketed the western valleys leading into the Yosemite Valley. In a meadow close to the Merced River a mule deer stood with velvety antlers. He lifted his head to look at the passing vehicles before turning and stepping cautiously back into the timber.

The Glacier Point road wound back and forth up the mountain range. Sheldon drove along, taking in the forest beauty and keeping his eyes peeled for more wildlife. His spirit was relaxed as he listened to Stanley and Howard arguing and the chatter of the girls in the back seat. Paul Rumble was driving ahead of him. *He sure is taking his good ol' time*, thought Sheldon impatiently.

When the youth arrived at the Glacier Point parking area, they unloaded their picnic supplies and hiked out to the point for their lunch. Spreading out the blankets they had brought along, the girls set out the sandwiches, cheeses, and vegetables. Sheldon set up his camera for a couple snapshots of his friends who were sprawled around talking and laughing. He snapped a few shots of Half Dome that loomed in the background. A group photo was also arranged for memory's sake.

After saying grace, the young people sat together and munched on their food. Even though it was noon, the altitude allowed them the pleasure of cool alpine air.

"I guess we'll be stuck at home for a while after this trip," said Donald, wiping his mouth with his hanky. "Since President Roosevelt requested to join the war, gas rationing is becoming mandatory. Gas, and also rubber. The military needs all the rubber and fuel they can get for their ships and planes."

"Yeah, and I heard they are now limiting how fast we should drive, too," said Howard Flory. "Thirty-five miles per hour. Ha!" he laughed. "I guess that's to save rubber."

The conversation about the effects of what would come to be known as World War II changed to local interests and day-to-day activities. Some of the young men stretched out and stared up into space as they listened to the girls talk about gardening, canning, dry yard experiences, and the latest sewing patterns. Sheldon watched a brightly colored Western tanager chase a female through the fir trees next to the sheer granite ledge.

"Let's sing a verse of 'What a Friend We Have in Jesus,' " suggested Mary Ellen as their chatter subsided. "Maybe we could sing the whole song since we all know it by heart."

"Sure, let's," said Stanley, gulping down the last of his drink. The sound of singing floated away on the afternoon breezes and a distant hawk swooped closer and turned his head. Sheldon sang along quietly and listened to the words and especially C.J. Rumble's daughter's voice as it reverberated across the clearing. She had picked the song and it had touched him. *She is beautiful and full of life. Just like the rest of God's creation.*

"Why don't we walk down Four-Mile Trail to shake down this food," suggested Paul after they had finished singing. "We can't come to Yosemite without walking a trail."

"Yessiree," said Donald. "Let's take our picnic things back to the vehicles before we set out. We won't have time to hike all the way, but at least we can enjoy a walk in the woods." The youth gathered their baskets and backpacks.

"Mary Ellen, we'll let you bring the two comforters," Vera laughed. "See you."

"Don't leave me behind with the bears." Mary Ellen feigned a scared look into the trees behind her.

"Oh well, Sheldon is still there and he can shoot it for you with his camera," Vera joked as she picked up her basket and jacket.

Sheldon took apart the camera stand and laid it beside his backpack. The other boys were already on their way back to the vehicles. He had taken a couple parting shots of the stunning mid-summer views of the Yosemite Valley and Sierra Peaks and paused a moment for a silent prayer. He picked up his things and turned to leave.

"Oh, sorry," he said as he nearly bumped into Mary Ellen. "I didn't know you were still here." Somehow he hadn't heard her walk across the stone shelf to stand near him. She had put the blankets beside her on the granite and was taking in the beauty.

"That's okay. The girls left me here with the bears." She continued to look out over the valley.

"Actually, I've been thinking . . ." began Sheldon.

"So you actually think!" Mary Ellen teased warmly. "Sometimes you're pretty quiet." Her smile and tremulous voice unnerved him.

Sheldon cleared his throat. "What I was going to say is a question." He turned to gaze across the expanse of the valley. A mockingbird landed on a branch a stone's throw away and began a different song.

"Isn't this beautiful," said Sheldon. He could hear the voices of the youth fading in the distance. The mockingbird hopped up to the next branch, then turned and continued to sing.

"Could I . . ."

"Another question?" smiled Mary Ellen.

"Could I see you?" blurted Sheldon.

"Can't you see me already?" she teased.

"Okay. Let me try again. May I see you with the intention of learning to know you better for the sole purpose of spending our lives together?" There, he had gotten it out. The mockingbird stopped singing; Sheldon imagined it was holding its breath just as he was.

"I think it would be great to learn to know you better. Your sister Vera told me you were interested," she said with a smile. "When can we start?"

"Now." Sheldon's heart left his throat and resumed its normal place. "Here, let me carry those blankets."

/ /

Temperatures soared as the sun climbed into the sky. Heat waves could be seen across the Stanislaus County as Sheldon walked to the end of the vineyard. He turned to look back at the acres of grapes he and his father had sulfured since early morning. It was time to stop this work now since the heat and sulfur together would burn the grapes and their leaves.

Even though grape farming was not his favorite activity, he still enjoyed the early mornings outdoors and the fresh San Joaquin Valley air. The grapevines were full of large green leaves and clusters of BB-sized grapes.

The past year has gone by so quickly, now that I have started seeing Mary Ellen, Sheldon thought. Now it was already June of 1943, and he was working hard to save every penny he could. He enjoyed working with Pop and with the hired help, but he looked forward to working together with his own wife and children. "Let's head back to the house, Sheldon," Pop hollered as he strode up and pitched the sulfur duster apparatus onto the pickup bed. He started the engine and revved it up. Sheldon laid his duster beside Pop's and got into the cab.

"So, what do you think about the Rumble girl by now?" asked Walter abruptly as he shoved the truck into gear and briskly bumped out onto Woodland Avenue. "Do you think she'll take you?"

"She's a wonderful person," answered Sheldon. "But her doctor told her the last time she was in to see him that she shouldn't get married because she has a congenital heart issue. He told her she might die giving birth."

"When did they discover that?" Pop frowned.

"Just very recently," said Sheldon gloomily.

"Hmm." Walter shifted down as he turned the corner.

"What do you think we should do?" asked Sheldon, glancing out the window as they passed Ransom School.

"Marry her, son, and love her. Let God take care of her and your future. Trust Him—that's my advice. But do as you think best."

The Chevy pickup rolled to a stop at home. The dust rose above the Goodyear tires on the slight draft and then settled.

"After we've eaten lunch, why don't we go over and see what Merven has going at the Johnson place," suggested Walter as he walked rapidly to the house. "He asked if we'd help the pickers this year with harvesting."

"Sure, Pop," replied Sheldon. His mind was not as much on the peach harvest as it was on the new turn of events with his girlfriend. *Why a heart problem? Should he consider someone else?* He had thought of this several times after Mary Ellen had told him the doctor's diagnosis. Today wasn't the first time it crossed his mind. What had Pop said? *Marry her, son, and love her and trust God.* He could never imagine himself with another girl. He would trust God to guide him. Enough thinking; the decision was made.

The week passed swiftly for Sheldon as he and his father worked together on their fruit farm and cared for the vineyards at both farms. Not only was there fruit to pick and vineyards to tend, there was also alfalfa hay to be put up. The hay needed to be cut and dried, then raked into mounds, forked onto wagons, and put into the barn. Some of the hay was sold to local farmers for their dairy cows, and some was saved for the Grovers' own livestock. Besides this, they also grew oats for their own livestock. There was always something to be done and no dull moments.

/ /

Friday evening came. Sheldon tilted his chair on its back legs and balanced there precariously. Vera tried to talk with him, but he was deep in thought and didn't even hear her.

 What to do about Mary Ellen Rumble? He didn't believe in dating just for fun. *Finding a life companion is more important than trying out partners to see which one is the most exciting. It is a serious undertaking, one that should be accompanied with prayer and fasting.* But what should he do about Mary Ellen's heart condition and their future? Even though he wanted to spend his life with her, the heart condition bothered him. Yet he did want to trust God through it all. Mixed feelings, someone had called it once. That's what it was.

Sheldon's chair came down with a *thump*. "Vera, would you like to go along with me to pick up Mary Ellen and go for ice cream? I think we'll go to Bluet's Ice Cream and then go for a drive along the river."

"Sure. Let me grab a sweater; the nights are cool down by the river." And with that the two were on their way.

"Hi, Sheldon," Mary Ellen slid in beside him and closed the car door. "It sure is clean in here. You always keep your car so nice and clean." She looked at him with admiration.

"Thank you." Sheldon wished his face wouldn't flush. It wasn't dignified. He shifted the car into gear and carefully let out the clutch. His car moved forward without the slightest lurch. He drove along slowly, enjoying the cool evening temperatures and the San Joaquin Valley countryside. Most of all he enjoyed just being with Mary Ellen. Sheldon enjoyed the outgoing nature of his girlfriend and felt safe with her in his presence. It was no wonder Vera also enjoyed being around her.

The wind reached in through the partially opened car windows and played with their hair. *I would never go out with another girl,* thought Sheldon. *Mary Ellen Rumble is a jewel.*

Sheldon steered his car off Hatch Road and out to the river's edge. They got out and walked along the river, talking. Vera soon wandered off, collecting wildflowers for a bouquet.

"I have enjoyed learning to know your family better," said Sheldon quietly. "And of course I have enjoyed learning to know you better, too." He surreptitiously rubbed sweaty palms along the sides of his trousers. "And I think I would like to spend my life with you." He held his breath, wondering how Mary Ellen would respond to his deepest feelings.

An osprey dipped down toward the river and hovered a moment before flying on. Somewhere an elk bugled. Shadows lengthened.

"So you would like to spend your life with me?" Mary Ellen bit her lip, gazing into Sheldon's sober face. "It makes me feel good to hear that. But what about my congenital heart problem?" Her voice was hesitant.

"I know." Sheldon couldn't tear his eyes away from her sweet face. Her glossy brown hair was tucked neatly under her head covering and her eyes were like dove's eyes. Pleading. "I asked my dad about that, and he thinks I should go ahead and trust God for the future." Sheldon thought he heard Mary Ellen sigh hopefully.

"If it's all right with you," he went on bravely, "let's continue seeing each other and keep moving forward unless the Lord shows He has a different path for us."

Mary Ellen's cheeks were delicately flushed and she lifted her eyes trustingly. "I think that sounds fine, Sheldon," she whispered. "That sounds like a good plan."

Sheldon arrived at home and parked his car. He crawled out and checked to make sure he wasn't parked too close to the fence to allow others to walk past.

Even though it was dark, a full moon was providing enough light to make shadows. He glanced at the house and could see that a light was still on in the living room. Someone must still be up—probably waiting on him and Vera.

He would take his time with Mary Ellen. *Maybe give it another year of waiting on God to see what He would have for him, and save a little money,* he thought. God would show him what to do. Anyway, no one knew when Christ would return. It could be anytime.

/ /

A couple of months later, Sheldon decided to take Mary Ellen out to Santa Cruz for a day. Vera and her friend Ruth would go along, and Sheldon asked Stanley Filbrun if he would go, too.

"Sure, I'll go," Stanley said in his good-natured way.

It was a partly cloudy, late summer morning when the five young people left for the ocean. Starting off early, Sheldon and Vera drove to each home and picked up their friends on the way out of Modesto. Sunrays pierced through the clouds periodically as they drove along the San Joaquin Valley at a good lick. They were enjoying each other's company and having a jolly good time.

"I hope we can get into the Gilda's Fish Restaurant on the wharf," said Vera.

"Why couldn't we?" Ruth swiveled her head to stare. "Think it will be too full to get into today, or what?"

"The food is so good that it's almost always full," Vera reminded her friend.

"The Stagnaro family began the restaurant in 1930 and have built a good business," commented Sheldon. "They also run the Stagnaro Sport Fishing fleet."

"Doesn't matter to me who owns it as long as the clam chowder is good," said Stanley with a sigh.

"Italians own it and Italians are known for their good food," said Sheldon. "Look out!" He slammed on the brakes as a Border collie herd dog chased a sheep off the highway.

It was late morning when the young people arrived at the Santa Cruz wharf. After Sheldon found a parking spot, they got out and stretched. Walking to the edge of the wharf, they watched sea lions playing in the water. Sea gulls dipped down to snatch food floating in the water along the wharf.

The wharf was opened for the purpose of shipping potatoes to San Francisco for mining camps in the Sierra Nevada during the gold rush. After the invention of vehicles and improved roads, the wharf became the base for the Monterey Bay fishing industry. During this time, Gilda's Fish Restaurant was opened by the Stagnaro family, who owned a thriving fishing company.

Sheldon watched the rise and fall of fishing boats in the bay as Mary Ellen leaned against the railing. They savored the cool Pacific air and breathed deeply of the ocean breeze. A hint of salt tingled in the air as the waves crashed against the wharf and tugged at the pilings. Palm trees along the wharf and beach bowed their heads to a gentle wind.

But despite the beautiful day and good company, Sheldon felt burdened. And maybe a bit restless. He wanted to be sure it was the Lord's will for him to marry Mary Ellen, but being patient wasn't one of his strong points. He liked to make things happen. But this decision would affect the rest of their lives. Could he make the decision, or should he wait until someone or something else made it for him?

chapter seven
TWO SHALL BE ONE

1944

Another year passed as Sheldon worked on the farm alongside his father and sometimes his grandfather Ira. He delighted in the times spent with the workers in the orchards and cutting yards as they picked, cut, cured, dried, and packaged peaches and apricots for the market. Grapes also were picked and transported to the winery.

And then there were the young people's outings and church functions to attend with Mary Ellen. Sunday morning services were also a weekly highlight and a spiritual stimulant. He especially enjoyed the occasional group discussions with the older brothers of the church who liked to discuss prophecies and end-time events.

"Daniel's prophetic voice gives us insight into end-time events," said Charles as he put down his coffee cup. "I believe we are in the end times."

"Even the words of Jesus give us an insight as to what is happening in our day," Ira's voice boomed. "If I recall correctly, He tells the women following

Him to Golgotha, 'Daughters of Jerusalem, weep not for me, but weep for yourselves, and for your children.'[1] And today, we can just look at what is happening over in Germany and Poland to these women's children, to their descendants." He shook his head soberly.

A number of families had been invited to Walter and Ida's home for Sunday lunch and now some of the men were having a discourse. A few of the women sat by and listened.

"The mass murdering of Jews in Europe is really terrible," agreed Walter. "The newspapers are saying millions are being destroyed."

"The prophecies of Christ are being fulfilled in our day," Charles said. "I believe God will reserve a remnant of Jews during the Great Tribulation, even though many have not yet accepted Jesus as Messiah."

The discussion moved on to other topics of interest to the men. More chairs were brought in and pushed into spots around the living room and kitchen area. The women and children squeezed in or sat in groups outside to talk. Windows were opened to let in the fresh valley air.

Sheldon sat next to the kitchen door listening to the conversations around him. Mary Ellen sat beside him, chatting with his sister Vera. The menfolk continued to talk about local and world news while some of the boys had a lively discussion concerning engines and horsepower.

"Why don't we go on a walk," suggested Mary Ellen quietly to Sheldon. Vera had gotten up to offer the guests more coffee and water, and the other young folks were engaged in conversations.

"Sure," Sheldon agreed readily. He was always ready for movement. He became restless when forced to sit too long. They stepped outside together. Groups of children played with each other among the redwood trees and around the cacti.

"Why don't we take a walk out to the orchard?" suggested Sheldon, and the two young people walked together across the wooden canal bridge and out through the dry yard to the orchard.

---

[1] Luke 23:28

After enjoying a walk across the farm and through the orchard, Sheldon and Mary Ellen turned back toward the homestead. It was a warm midsummer day with a little breeze blowing south from the Pacific.

"Let's walk over to the house where Merven and Pauline used to live," Sheldon said. The small two-room-and-shed cabin had been put up about a year after they married. They lived there until they moved over to the Esther Johnson place.

Sheldon and Mary Ellen explored the little cabin just to the west of Grandpa Ira's house. Cobwebs hung from the corners and dust lay everywhere, showing that the inhabitants had not been there for some time. Sheldon opened the woodshed and peered into the lean-to. A few pieces of wood remained forgotten in the corner.

"This could be livable with a bit of tender loving care," said Mary Ellen. She smiled up at Sheldon. "Don't you think so?"

"I think it could be cleaned and fixed to be very nice, but maybe not as nice as what you are used to."

"Oh, Sheldon." Her voice held gentle reproof. "It doesn't matter where we live if we have each other."

"So are you saying that you would marry me?" Sheldon closed the door to the woodshed carefully and glanced around to make sure they were alone. It wouldn't do for any random passer-by to overhear this conversation. And the way his heart was pounding in his ears, he wanted to make sure he was hearing right.

"Of course I would marry you! I don't want to live with anyone else. I want you." Mary's eyes shone.

Sheldon thought about the doctor's recommendation. *She shouldn't get married because she has a congenital heart issue. She might die giving birth.* His brain whirled. Then came his father's advice: *Marry her, son, and love her. Let God take care of her and your future. Trust Him.*

"Yes," said Sheldon quietly. "I want you to be my wife. I want to marry you and provide for you as long as I live." He leaned against the shed and crossed his arms. His grin stretched from ear to ear. "How shall we announce it?"

Mary Ellen stood next to Sheldon among the weeds and wildflowers that surrounded the little cabin. The breeze played with a wisp of hair that had escaped her covering.

"Why don't you take some photos and get Vera to use some of her artistic skills to make an announcement?"

"That sounds like a good idea." Sheldon smiled into Mary Ellen's blue eyes. "When should we have a wedding? Any suggestions?"

"Let's talk with our parents and ask them," said Mary Ellen.

Walking back the way they had come, the two young people could hear the voices and laughter of visitors of all ages. Sharing a look, they added their own joyful laughter to the afternoon.

The next few months were exciting ones for Sheldon and Mary Ellen as they conferred with their families concerning the wedding plans. The big day would be September 27, 1944.

Often a German Baptist wedding was held at the home of the bride's parents or at a community building. After some discussion, it was decided to have the wedding at the home of Mary Ellen's parents. In addition to the normal workload, cleaning, organizing, and repairing at Joseph and Flossie Rumble's homestead kept everyone very busy preparing for the special day. New rugs were bought for some of the rooms and a fresh coat of paint applied to give the already lovely home a fresh look. Hired hands helped plant a few new bushes and flower beds around the exterior of the place, creating a pleasing appearance.

Meanwhile, Sheldon also found time to work on the little house his brother had once occupied with his own bride. First, he thoroughly cleaned both the inside and outside to remove all the cobwebs, dust, and mouse litter. With the help of his father, he repaired some of the flooring and the ceiling covering that had worked itself loose over the years. The house wasn't very airtight and at some splices light shone through the cracks. Mary Ellen, Vera, and Ruth Cover worked on making new curtains and Ida and Grandma Maggie knotted comforters for the bed.

The two-room cabin soon began to take on the appearance of a cozy little home, in need only of a small family to live there. The floors were repaired and a few spots sanded and polished. New wallpaper covered the living room area. A stove that would serve as a wood burner, cook stove, and water heater stood polished and cold.

Sheldon cut weeds and cleared a path leading to the old outhouse so he could do repairs on this little building too. *It sure is a blessing to have so much help from our families and friends,* he thought as he worked. *How else would we be able to renovate, clean, and prepare for the wedding?* He was thankful to be a part of a brotherhood whose members practiced community and sharing.

Even though time was taken for wedding preparation, the peach and apricot harvest needed to continue. Long days were the norm as Sheldon and his father worked on the farm and over at the Woodland Avenue orchards. Merven also needed their help at his orchard on Hatch Road south of the Tuolumne River, so everyone worked from sunup to sundown.

Some evenings Sheldon worked after it got dark, cutting the firewood he and Mary Ellen would need for cooking and for heat during the cooler months of winter. Even though the winters were not normally frigid in the San Joaquin Valley, a fire kept the chill off and gave them a place to huddle. He swiftly cut and split blue gum and some fruitwood and then wheeled it to the lean-to woodshed and stacked it full. Splitting and carrying wood heats you twice, as Grandpa Ira would say; once when it's split and once when it's burned.

During their engagement, Sheldon and Mary Ellen enjoyed times together reading the Scriptures and praying. They wanted God's blessing upon their future and their home, especially during these years of uncertainty and economic depression. Even though the economy was better, the government called for mandatory rationing of almost every product and food so the surplus could be sent to the soldiers fighting in Europe. Time spent together in the Word of God helped build their faith despite the economic trouble around them.

When Sheldon and his fiancée were not together planning the wedding or preparing the cabin, Mary Ellen would spend time with her mother, Flossie.

She and her mother laughed and talked together as they sewed clothing and dresses for the bride-to-be. A special white fabric was purchased for Mary Ellen's wedding dress. There were still household duties and washing and baking to be done during this period, which brought Mary Ellen back down to earth from her dreams. Sometimes her brothers Dale and Paul teased her about sleeping while she worked. "Or maybe it's dreaming with your eyes open," Dale would say. "You are not engaged with us anymore since you announced your engagement," he teased.

Early on Wednesday morning, the day of his wedding, Sheldon found himself whistling when he got up to shower and prepare for the special day. He had his clothes packed to go to Mt. Herman, where they planned to go for their wedding trip. Mt. Herman was a Christian conference center with many little cabins in the redwoods near Santa Cruz. He and Mary Ellen planned to stay at a friend's cabin for a week.

After a good breakfast by his mother, a last meal with his family, he prepared to leave. He bade farewell to his parents and Vera and picked up his suitcase.

"See you at the wedding, Sheldon," said Mama. "Daddy and I and Vera will be coming over soon." Her eyes glistened as she watched her son gather his belongings.

The sun was peeking above the Sierra Mountain range as Sheldon's sedan rumbled along Dakota Avenue. *Such a beautiful day for a wedding,* he thought, humming a favorite hymn.

When Sheldon arrived at the Rumbles, Mary Ellen came breezing out of the house. He opened his car door and stepped out.

"Wow, you look handsome," his bride flirted just a bit. "I am not ready yet but come in and make yourself at home. Do you want a cup of tea?" Her smile was like the morning sunshine and her eyes sparkled. She was dressed in a light blue dress with darker blue polka dots.

"I think you look great anytime." Sheldon smiled at her, heart swelling with joy. "Let me grab my suit coat."

The two walked together in silence. They stopped momentarily to enjoy the sweet smell of chrysanthemums mixed with the acrid tang of hulled almonds that hung over them.

Some of the rooms were filled with benches and a special place toward the center of the house was set up with seating for Sheldon and Mary Ellen and their parents. The ministers also had a place to sit nearby. Guests began to arrive and more were invited impromptu. Soon the families were seated and singing began. A quartet of friends stood on a balcony for special singing. A sermon was preached from Ephesians 5 and the wedding ceremony performed by Minister Joseph Rumble, Mary Ellen's father.

"Alvah Sheldon Grover, will you take Mary Ellen Rumble, the sister by your side, to be your wedded wife? Will you love and cherish her, provide and care for her . . ."

Following the exchange of vows, Joseph prayed for them. "God, bless this new home. Be a central part of this young couple's life and home. Help them be faithful to the vows they have just made."

Then the couple was presented to the guests as Mr. and Mrs. Sheldon Grover. The mothers wiped their eyes, smiling tremulously.

Wedding photos were taken for memory's sake and some of their closest friends served a wedding cake, mixed nuts, as well as something to drink. It was a delightful time for family and friends to enjoy fellowship and celebrate the marriage of two of their young people. It was always a happy occasion when another Christian home was formed.

After the reception, which included lots of warm fellowship and hugs from their parents and siblings, Sheldon and Mary Ellen Grover were off. Everyone waved as the newlyweds pulled out to leave for their wedding trip.

Sheldon and Mary Ellen Grover on their wedding day.

"It was really a beautiful day, wasn't it?" sighed Mary Ellen as she laid her hand on Sheldon's arm. He had thrown his suit coat and vest onto the back seat and had rolled up his sleeves. She admired his lithe, wiry strength. Just because he was quiet did not mean he was not thinking.

"I liked the cake—it was perfect. And so was everything else." Sheldon's eyes twinkled. "But the preferred part of the wedding was you."

They drove along laughing and sharing memories of their dating days and the wedding. They dreamed about the future and their plans to raise a family if God permitted. Farming orchards was also a part of Sheldon's dream, a work that now included Mary Ellen too. He had proven that he could marry a Rumble and he had finally "gotten his queen," as his friend Don Beachler had remarked to him at the wedding.

They stopped at a filling station along the way to buy a bottle of cold Coke and to relax. As they sipped their colas, cars rumbled by and trucks blew their horns in frustration at the traffic. An attendant jumped back and raised his voice at a motorist who pulled up too fast and close to the gas pump.

Sheldon and Mary Ellen arrived at Mt. Herman and set up camp at the Nyquist cabin. They had brought along some food that Flossie and Ida had packed for the trip. Sheldon had brought his camera but not much else since everything else they might need was stored at the cabin. It was only early evening so there was plenty of light for a walk in the redwoods.

"Oh no," exclaimed Mary Ellen. "I forgot to bring my suitcase along!"

"Are you sure?" asked Sheldon, opening the trunk of the car to double check.

"I remember thinking about it before we left and I was going to ask you to take it for me, but somehow I forgot." She groaned. "I guess I will be wearing my wedding dress for a week."

They both laughed to think of hiking through the woods or on the railroad in a beautiful white wedding gown.

"No," said Sheldon. "We will go into Santa Cruz tomorrow and we'll buy some clothes there. We will call Merven when we are in town and perhaps they can bring your suitcase."

The next day the young couple slept later than usual. When they finally got up and prepared for the day, it was mid-morning. They ate a breakfast of cold cereal and knelt to ask for God's blessing on their day. Then they drove to Santa Cruz for some clothing for the bride and to make an important phone call back home.

chapter eight
CPS CAMP DAYS

1944–1946

"Dear," said Sheldon as he stepped into the house. "I think we just received something important from the Selective Service."

"Oh, no." Mary Ellen dropped her head into her hands. "Don't tell me they are drafting you." She leaned against him to look at the paper he held.

"Selective Service System, ORDER TO REPORT FOR INDUCTION, The President of the United States, To Alvah Sheldon Grover. Greeting: You are hereby ordered for induction into the Armed Forces of the United States, and to report at . . ."

It was not easy for Mary Ellen to face the thought of living without Sheldon, but she knew with God's divine enablement she would manage. At least she had his parents and grandparents just a stone's throw away.

"Remember the verse in Philippians 4:13," Sheldon comforted her. "'I can do all things through Christ which strengtheneth me.'"

Sheldon was able to obtain Classification 1-O, a provision for men opposed to serving the military in any capacity. He was not the only young German Baptist getting an induction notice. Mary Ellen's two brothers Dale and Paul, as well as Stanley Filbrun, were also sent draft notices, as well as other young men from the community. Thankfully all of them were able to get Conscientious Objector status in the alternative service program.

Sheldon would be serving at the Civilian Public Service (CPS) Camp 134 near Belden, California. This camp was a Forest Service unit operated by the Brethren Service Committee, opened in May 1944. The men put out forest fires, maintained and repaired equipment, and performed fire prevention tasks. Timber cruising, which was measuring trees for lumber, was also a duty of the CPS boys.

On the morning of December 6, 1944, Sheldon and Mary Ellen spent extra time together in prayer and Scripture reading. After enjoying a delicious breakfast together and holding each other close for a long time, they finally said their good-byes. Sheldon, loading his suitcase and camera bag into the car, waved goodbye to his wife. Mary Ellen smiled bravely and waved, but ran into the house to cry as soon as the car was out of sight. This was a scene repeated across the church communities as young men upheld their non-resistant beliefs.

Sheldon first drove by the Filbruns to pick up Stanley, who also needed to go to the CPS camp at Belden. They drove north from Modesto and travelled through the Sacramento Valley for several hours. Soon they left the valley and headed up Dark Canyon Road, northeast along the Feather River, and then to a bridge which crossed to the far side of the canyon. The gravel roads wound back through the mountains along the Feather River and through several tunnels. The roads were fairly well maintained by the conservation and road department even though they were a good distance away from civilization. Their drive took them through the heavily timbered Plumas Forest. CPS Camp 134 was nestled among the Sierra Nevada Mountain Range just south of the Cascade Ranges.

They arrived at camp and registered and then were shown their sleeping quarters. After unpacking they stepped outside to find the directors and other COs (Conscientious Objectors) discussing future activities and plans for the camp.

A few of the boys were sent to work in the garden and others were given the job of splitting wood. Two young men were sent to fix a cabin roof.

The days seemed to drag by for Sheldon as he imagined himself back on the farm working in the orchard and living with Mary Ellen. He had hoped to work hard and save enough money to build or buy Mary Ellen a nicer place. She had been used to living in better conditions than a little cabin. But they would manage, he supposed. They had been together only two months before he was drafted. *I guess all things work together for good*, Sheldon thought as he split another piece of wood. *At least I am enjoying the work assignments.*

Director Williams let the young men know that each month they would have two days' leave if they wanted it. "And these furlough days may also be accumulated," he had said. "If you want to wait three months you may have six days of furlough." This was mighty good news to a newlywed!

/ /

"Sheldon, I am not feeling the best again," murmured Mary Ellen at the breakfast table. "I need to lie down for a moment, please."

"I'll wash the dishes," offered Sheldon as he rose to clean the table. He busied himself with washing the dishes and setting them up to dry. He wiped the tabletop and hung the rag on the hook.

Sheldon had saved up a four-day furlough, and he was enjoying every minute spent with his wife.

"Will you be okay if I go out for a while? Pop thought I might like to help spray the orchard today." Sheldon knelt beside his wife. Her eyes flickered open for a moment.

"I should be okay. I just need to rest." She closed her eyes again. "Maybe I overdid it yesterday when I helped Mama clean." Sheldon remained next to the couch a few minutes longer before leaving the house.

Eight months had passed since their wedding day. Life was fresh and young, and after returning from Mt. Herman they had soon fallen into the routine of working together as husband and wife. Whether it was cleaning house or working outdoors, they often helped each other. But only two months after they were married, the induction notice had changed their lives.

When Sheldon returned later that morning, Mary Ellen was up and busy with the laundry. The electric Maytag ringer washer was churning the clothing. The washer had been a wedding present from their Rumble parents. The "good ole' days" of hauling nearly fifty gallons of water to boil, wash, and rinse one batch of clothing were now history. Gone too were the weary days of rubbing clothes on a washboard, of wringing and lifting heavy waterlogged clothing. They were thankful for the time and energy they could save by using the new washing machine.

They strung a line between the house and a nearby blue gum tree on which they hung their wash. When Sheldon was close by he often carried the wash basket out to the line for his wife. He loved to listen to Mary Ellen relate news from her parents or someone else in the community she had spoken with. Or sometimes she would ask him how things were going on the farm.

The next couple of days were exciting ones for Sheldon and Mary Ellen. They were sure that Mary Ellen's nausea was a result of her first pregnancy. They would be expecting their first child in December if the pregnancy went well.

"To think that before we are born, God knows our future," remarked Sheldon. "In Jeremiah 1:5 it says, 'Before I formed thee in the belly I knew thee; and before thou camest forth out of the womb I sanctified thee, and I ordained thee a prophet unto the nations.' "

The weekend passed, and soon it was Monday—and time for Sheldon to head back to camp. It hurt him to leave Mary Ellen at home alone in her condition, but law was law. *I am just grateful to God that I am allowed alternative service,* he thought as he paused for a minute to gaze across the beckoning farm and orchards. *And God will continue to care for my wife at home.*

"Goodbye, Sheldon," said Mary Ellen. She leaned into the car window to kiss him goodbye.

It was noon before Sheldon drove into the camp at Belden and parked his car. He gathered his belongings and the food Mary Ellen had packed for him and then checked in with Director Williams to receive his instructions for the afternoon. *Unpack, settle in, and appear at the mess hall to help with the evening meal,* Williams had said. Sheldon had also brought back a trunk full of goods from some of the church folks, and he unloaded this at the mess hall, too.

The camp was quiet except for a few cooks and the director. Wind moaned through the fir and pine trees that bowed their heads over the dormitories where the COs normally slept. During the afternoon, Sheldon helped the camp dietitian and the young men who had been assigned as cooks. The rest of the afternoon he spent working in the garden plot where they raised some of their own food. Little did he know how well those gardening skills would serve him in later years, although his methods would change to suit sadly altered circumstances.

The CO men normally worked nine hours a day, six days a week, fighting fires and maintaining equipment. Sheldon enjoyed working in the mountain ranges, in the great outdoors. He learned to identify more trees, wildflowers, herbs, insects, and animals during his time in the forests. Douglas firs, incense cedars, black oaks, and ponderosa pines created a dense forest over much of the terrain and often they would see squirrels, rabbits, and mule deer bounding for cover. Lots of other forest animals were recorded as the boys waded through underbrush and cleared paths. On occasion, they went fishing in the mountain streams and lakes.

When a call came in for a forest fire, they would jump onto the trucks and tear along the gravel roads to the site of the fire, yank on their big overcoats, and pile off into the forest. The young men would stomp through underbrush to chop and clear paths and start backfires. They would search the ground for any hotspots and squirt water from their backpack water-tanks onto any remaining smolders. Powdery white ash swirled into the air and was carried away by the wind. By evening, they would be exhausted with fighting, covered with soot and dirt, and saturated with the smell of smoke.

Stumbling back to the makeshift campsites, they would devour what the cooks had prepared: steak, potatoes, tomatoes, bread, butter and jam and, on occasion, fruit. Falling asleep was never a problem for the firefighters. They could roll in a blanket near the campfire or curl up in a tent and sleep soundly while the owls called mournfully and Pacific tree frogs sang together.

Sometimes Sheldon would lie in his bedroll at night and listen to the chorus and dream about the future. He wished he could get out of these camps and back into his life of climbing up the rungs of success instead of simply climbing mountains. World War II was putting a halt to his ambitious race for the top. But surely it wouldn't last too much longer and he would be out with his wife and pushing for his goals.

But during the day his mind was kept busy with work and accountability to the camp directors. He enjoyed the hard work and banter alongside his German Baptist brothers. Most of all he looked forward to Sunday—a day off.

Sunday was a day of worship and recreation for the men in camp. The director, who also served as pastor at times, would lead out with singing, a Scripture reading and sermon, and prayer at the end. If there was no pastor, the COs would organize a worship service among themselves. Often, they would spend the rest of the day relaxing and fellowshipping or writing letters to the folks back home.

On one occasion, Mary Ellen came to the camp along with some of the young people from the community. The young men in camp had brothers and sisters who wanted to see how and where the COs lived.

Mary Ellen brought Sheldon new socks and another jacket. With all the walking and climbing, he was glad for her gifts.

"Sounds like we 'Modestors' are being transferred to Three Rivers soon," said Dale one evening at camp. The Modesto boys were preparing for bed after a hard day. They had returned to the main camp, showered, and eaten a good meal.

"I'm okay with that," said Stanley. "I'm ready to see something new anyway."

"Yes, but I heard it's way back in no man's land." Paul yanked his blanket back and jumped into bed.

"You think Merven will still ship that box of fruit to you way out there in the hills, Sheldon?" Eldon hinted wistfully. Every week Sheldon's brother Merven sent a twenty-pound box packed full of fresh peaches, apricots, and nectarines to him and Stanley, Pauline's brother. Sometimes Merven would also send a large crock of olives he had cured.

"We have lots of friends on the day that box comes, don't we?" Sheldon looked at Stanley with a wry grin.

It wasn't long before the young German Baptist men from Modesto were transferred to CPS Camp No. 107, a National Park Service camp operated by MCC (Mennonite Central Committee) and positioned at Three Rivers, California. This camp, hidden deep in the forests near the entrance of the Sequoia National Park, was 35 miles from the nearest town of Visalia. At the Three Rivers camp, the men not only fought forest fires but also repaired trails and maintained roads. A few of the men also worked as stonemasons. Some helped stock mountain streams with fish.

In the evenings the young men would talk about the day's events or news about the war, most of all when it would end. Sometimes the men would discuss the Scriptures and some were more passionate than others about such things. The Selective Service camp in the Trinity Alps where Sheldon had served for a while was mostly made up of men who would not cooperate at other government CPS camps, and there the men avoided spiritual topics. But at the MCC camp at Three Rivers a larger variety of denominations, including the vocal Russian Molokans, often caused their debates to become heated.

Sheldon was glad he was able to work with some of the young men from his own community. At night he slept in a cot next to Don Beachler and Don Miller. A number of the other German Baptist young men were also transferred to this camp.

Many German Baptist young men were at CPS camps during this time, some of whom were married. Merven Grover proposed that the brotherhood create a fund for these young men. The proposal was accepted and at the council meetings each year they took up offerings for this fund. After the war ended, this money was dispersed to the returning COs, based on how much time they had spent in camp. Some of the men received up to one thousand dollars, which was a great asset in helping them restart their lives at home.

One day in late December when Sheldon had come back to the mess hall for lunch with his unit, the camp director approached him. Sheldon and the rest of the men from his unit had been out lumber cruising—collecting data about local trees—near the Three Rivers Camp.

"I have a message for you," Wayne Book said as he handed Sheldon a note. Sheldon read the paper.

> *Dear Sheldon,*
>
> *We have a son—born December 27. Can you come home for a few days? We would love to see you.*
>
> *Mary Ellen*

Sheldon's heart leapt. Of course he wanted to see his son! If only he could have been there to enjoy the first moments with Mary Ellen. At least he had a furlough saved up, a four-day one. He could hardly wait.

Director Book agreed for Sheldon to start his leave the next day, a Saturday. He would need to be back before noon on Wednesday of the next week. Sheldon was excited as he drove out of Three Rivers the next morning along the winding gravel roads to civilization. Dust boiled up behind his car as he motored along. Even though it often rained this time of year, it was still dry in these southern mountains.

As Sheldon drove home, he thought about his future. How could he teach his little son if he wasn't at home? When could he go back to raising a godly family and working with his orchards and vineyards? What if this war was part of end-time events? Maybe his tiny son would be part of the last generation to be born before the Lord returned. It surely had to be soon.

chapter nine
SHADOW OF DEATH

1947–1951

In August 1946, after the war ended, Sheldon was released from CPS camp to return to Modesto. He was delighted about joining Mary Ellen and little Mark and living on the farm. Sheldon could not remember the route home taking that long, but maybe he was just more excited than usual. After all, he had been away from his home longer than he had expected.

Sheldon had called Mary Ellen and told her the good news, so she could be prepared for his arrival. Sure enough, late in the afternoon as Sheldon rolled up Shoemake Avenue, he could see that Mary Ellen was waiting at the end of the long lane with a little boy in her arms. Tears welled up in Sheldon's eyes as his little family came into view. When he finally arrived, he turned into the drive and stopped. Before he could open the door, Mary Ellen yanked it open and jumped into his arms. She clung to Sheldon while little Mark beat on his chest.

Sheldon wiped a tear from his cheek and pulled Mark into the car.

"How's my little boy?" he whispered.

"Da-da," he answered, touching Sheldon's face with his tiny finger.

"We are so-o-o glad to see you," said Mary Ellen. "You can't imagine how happy we are!"

Sheldon had spent nearly two years in CPS camps in four locations with only a few days for a leave now and then. Even though it was cloudy and had rained that morning, the little Grover family was in good spirits.

"Let's get into the car," said Mary Ellen, sliding into the passenger's seat and pulling Mark into her lap. "We are having an evening meal at your parents' house. As soon as you called, we planned a celebration." She gave his arm a squeeze and snuggled close. Sheldon drove to his parents' house and parked.

"So how does it feel to be back home in Modesto?" Ira smiled at his grandson and his family.

"You have no idea how good it is." Sheldon's reply was fervent. "It is so good to see everyone. And how have you and Grandma been, Grandpa?" he asked.

"I am doing well but Mother is feeling her age. But God is good to us."

The Grover family celebrated Sheldon's return with smoked turkey, cranberry sauce, and sweet tea. Sheldon's mom also served fruit and nuts. The best part was just enjoying the close proximity of relatives and friends. Sheldon told stories of camp days and showed some of the photos he had taken. It was so good to have all the family together again.

"We should be going home, Sheldon," said Mary Ellen. "Mark is getting fussy. It's past his bedtime."

"I guess you'll have to learn that you are not by yourself anymore, Sheldon." Walter gave his son a hearty slap on the shoulder. He yawned noisily. "Now you have a child to take care of."

Sheldon and Mary Ellen bade the family goodbye and stepped out into the darkening night. At home, Mary Ellen tucked Mark in bed and Sheldon unloaded the car. Soon they too were settled down for the night.

The next day Sheldon took a walk across the farm to check out the orchards and vineyard. He also rode over to Woodland Avenue to investigate the vineyards and orchards there. Mary Ellen and Mark rode along.

It wasn't long before Sheldon was back into the routine of family life and orcharding. It was so wonderful to be home again. He understood better than ever before the value of a godly wife, a warm meal, and a home of one's own. With training his young son, listening to and caring for his wife, and checking on his grandparents next door, Sheldon seemed to stay busy.

During the spring and summer of 1947, Sheldon needed to take more time out for Mary Ellen again since they were now expecting their second child. Ida also came over as needed to mind fifteen-month-old Mark.

Sheldon's father and Merven, with the help of some brothers from church, had kept the orchards and vineyards in good shape while he was away. The pruning had been done, the orchards raked clean, and the drying trays repaired. The work was primed and waiting.

Sometimes Sheldon would take Mark along with him to the orchards and dream about a time when they would raise and harvest fruit together. *Not only do I want to teach my children how to work diligently,* he thought, *but also how to persevere when things go wrong.* It had been tough during the Depression days and the war, and they had worked hard just to survive.

Sheldon was determined to build his business and to provide for his family. He wasn't as husky as some men, but he had determination and he was good at coming up with strategies for getting ahead financially.

He also wanted to strengthen the walls of Zion by being a faithful member of the church and a consistent follower of Jesus. There would always be areas where he could grow spiritually—he was certain of that. He wanted to be steady in how he lived, so that God could depend on him. *Oh, that I might live to make your name great, Lord,* he prayed.

He worried about his sister Frieda and her husband. They were not doing well in their marriage since Delmer wasn't always faithful. Delmer spent lots of money on his bad habits, so that meant they were also struggling financially. And now Delmer was disfellowshipped from the church because he was living a sinful life. Sheldon wished he could do more for his hurting sister—but what?

He was glad that Vera's husband, Donald Miller, worked hard and provided for their family. Though he might not have excelled academically, Donald had strength of character and he worked hard in his construction business. He wasn't rich, but he had enough money to keep bread on the table and help others in need.

And then there was Merven; Sheldon considered his brother a true deacon. Not only was he ordained in the Tuolumne church in that role, but he also acted like one. He worked hard. He helped poor Dust Bowl refugees by giving them jobs in his orchards. His truly was a rags-to-riches story. And like Donald, he loved to give.

Sheldon cared deeply about his family, even though he might not express it easily. *Seems all of us Grover men are sort of gruff ol' characters,* he thought with some chagrin. *Maybe something will soften me up one of these days.*

/ /

"Sheldon," murmured Mary Ellen. It was the wee hours of an October morning. The moon had collaborated with the window to throw a square of light on their bed.

"What?" Sheldon sat up and rubbed his eyes.

"I'm sure I'll need to go to the hospital this morning. You should let our mothers know." She lay back down again, breathing heavily.

Later that day at the hospital, a little girl was born to Sheldon and Mary Ellen. They named her Marilyn. A healthy baby, the doctor had said, and there were no complications.

Jenny, a lady originally from Holland but now living in Modesto, was willing to come and work as a maid for a small fee. She loved the children and would help with the laundry and cleaning. A few times Jenny even rolled up the carpets and took them outside by herself to beat them clean. She was every bit of six feet tall and tougher than nails. Sometimes she would make meals if Mary Ellen wasn't feeling up to it.

Life became busier with two children but Sheldon wouldn't have chosen anything different. He enjoyed holding his little daughter in one arm and Mark in the other. *Father, bless these two,* he prayed, *and guide their little feet on the path of righteousness. Lead them not into temptation but protect and keep them for thy kingdom's sake.*

Sheldon built a merry-go-round out of an old wooden wagon wheel. Mark would sit on the horizontal wheel and Sheldon or Mary Ellen would give it a hearty spin.

"Some more," he would giggle while clinging tightly to the slowing wheel.

In the redwood grove, Grandpa Walter had built a swing on which the children also played. Two redwood trees stood like giant sentinels just west of the barn, and between these two was the swing. The wind gently moved the board and rope when the swing was not in use. Sheldon loved to push his children and hear their cries of delight. The swing could also be pumped by the children to go higher and higher until there was enough slack in the rope at the top for the swinging child to drop down dangerously.

As Mark and Marilyn grew older and began playing together outdoors, they frequented the swing or the merry-go-round and made paths through the weeds and wildflowers along the redwoods. Sometimes they stood and watched the workers in the cutting shed. They also liked to sit on the edge of the canal and splash their feet in the moving water. Mary Ellen or Jenny, the maid, would sit nearby and watch.

"Be careful, children," Mary Ellen would say. "We need the water but it can be dangerous."

Sheldon spent time in the evenings with Mary Ellen and the children. He would study the Scriptures and pray with the family as his father had. Sometimes he read a Bible story to Mark and Marilyn before praying together and putting them to bed.

Prophecy was a topic Sheldon continued to explore and muse upon. *What does Matthew say? "But of that day and hour knoweth no man, no, not the angels of heaven, but my Father only,"*[1] he thought. *We have no need to fear the Second Coming, but rather we can anticipate the trumpet sound and the coming of the Lord with joy. Lord, prepare me for that coming day,* he prayed.

---

[1] Matthew 24:36

Whatever it takes, I want to be ready.

Sometimes Sheldon would flip through a new issue of *National Geographic* during the cooler winter evenings, while Mary Ellen read a Golden Book to Mark and Marilyn. It was relaxing to hear Mary Ellen's gentle voice as she read, the chatter and oohing of the children as they pointed at the pictures, and the snapping of fire in the woodstove that he had just stoked with dry fruit wood.

Life was back to normal for Sheldon and Mary Ellen as they farmed, taught their children, and helped encourage and build the body of Christ.

In the summer of 1949, Mary Ellen once again found herself heavy with child and often stopping to rest or lying in bed. Their first two children were born with few or no complications in spite of her heart problem.

Hopefully this birth will go as well as the first two, thought Sheldon as he pushed a rail car to the sulfur shed. *Maybe the doctor wasn't right. Father,* he prayed, *bless Mary Ellen with a good birth.*

The sun burned down upon Sheldon and the fruit pickers as they harvested the peaches and apricots. Vehicles bumped across the canal bridge around the barn and passed the redwood grove to the dry yard and cutting shed. Dust swirled as the harvesting crew helped pick peaches, while others cut and lay the fruit on trays. Don Miller helped haul peaches from Woodland orchard to the cutting shed on Shoemake.

Sometimes while Sheldon was busy with the orcharding and harvest, Mary Ellen would take the two youngest children for a doctor's appointment. She liked it better when Sheldon was along but sometimes this was not possible.

One evening in September during the latter part of the peach harvest, Sheldon came in from the orchards. He washed his hands at the sink and found the table set with tableware and the evening meal. Mark and Marilyn played quietly on the living room floor with a wooden truck and a homemade doll.

"Mary Ellen," called Sheldon. "I'm back." There was no answer. Sheldon hurried to their bedroom and pushed open the door. Mary Ellen was lying over the bed. She was still.

"Mary Ellen, dear, what's wrong?" Sheldon gently shook her.

Her eyes opened momentarily and closed again.

"Dear, are you okay?" Sheldon felt her face and hands. They were warm.

"I made supper," she faintly replied. "It's on the table. I may need to go to the hospital soon."

Sheldon quickly called his mother and then helped his wife get ready to leave. Ida came over and fed the children the soup that was cooling on the table. Soon Sheldon and Mary Ellen were on their way. Sheldon chewed his lip as he drove as fast as he safely could.

Oh Father, he prayed, *please take care of my dear wife.* They arrived at the Memorial Hospital in Ceres in good time and checked in. Soon the nurses had Mary Ellen taken to a room. The smell of antiseptic and medicines was not something Sheldon liked. It reminded him of suffering and depression. *But I suppose someone needs to work here,* he thought. The friendly attitudes of the nurses and other hospital staff helped make the environment bearable.

A few hours into the evening, the doctor recommended that Sheldon go home to his family until they called with more news on how the birth was going.

"Get a good night's sleep," the doctor smiled. "We'll see you in the morning." Sheldon had no choice but to leave his wife for the night. He gave Mary Ellen a reassuring hug.

"I'll be praying," he said as he got up. She smiled faintly and closed her eyes.

As Sheldon drove through Modesto, he prayed aloud. After arriving home, he told his mother how the evening had gone and thanked her for coming to mind the children. "I may need you or someone to watch the little ones again tomorrow," he said. That night, Sheldon tossed and turned, lonely and troubled.

In the morning, Sheldon had just gotten Mark and Marilyn their breakfast when the phone rang. He grabbed it on the first ring.

"You have a baby girl, and the mother seemed to do well," said the nurse who called. "You can come and see your newborn baby." Sheldon wanted to ask a question, but the line had already gone dead. His shoulders lifted slightly as if a burden had just rolled off.

"You have a new sister, children!" he boomed joyfully.

Sheldon called Mary Ellen's parents to let them know and then took Mark and Marilyn over to his mother so she could watch them until he returned. Soon he was on his way to the hospital. When he arrived, he checked in and found Mary Ellen's room.

Sheldon sat down and waited for the nurse to return. Mary Ellen was sleeping. Somewhere he heard a baby cry. Was that his daughter? The door pushed open and the nurse returned, pushing a small bundle into Sheldon's hands. He pulled back the little blanket to uncover another cute little girl. Mary Ellen and he had decided on the name Rebecca if it was a girl.

The minutes ticked by as he sat on the padded wooden chair with Rebecca. The baby squirmed and blinked, then relaxed. The doctor stepped into the room.

"Your wife pulled through again, Sheldon. Her physical condition isn't ideal, but she seems to be doing well." He rubbed his receding hairline. "You need to take care of her. She's a good woman."

After the doctor left, a nurse came to take baby Rebecca, or "Becky," for a diaper change and a bottle. Sheldon drove home. He stopped by his parents to tell Mark and Marilyn about their little sister Becky.

The next day Mary Ellen was discharged from the hospital and Sheldon went to get her and the newborn. He was overjoyed at the successful birth and the tiny little girl who was his second daughter. Before long, Mary Ellen would have two good helpers in the house to help her with household chores and cooking. He praised the Lord for a healthy family.

Post-partum depression was an unfamiliar term in those days, but it became a well-known reality in their home after Becky's birth. Unfortunately, this would be a nagging problem for Mary Ellen for a long time.

The fall of 1949 had brought a necessary change; it was time for Sheldon and Mary Ellen's oldest child to start school. Mark would need to start in kindergarten at Salida because Ransom School on Shoemake didn't have a kindergarten. When Mary Ellen felt well enough, she carpooled with three other mothers who had girls Mark's age—Virginia Miller, Judy Lynch, and Sharon Dunlap.

Another two years passed, with Mary Ellen and Sheldon working hard and caring for their little ones. One morning, Sheldon headed for the cutting shed where he was repairing trays, and Mary Ellen started the household chores.

Around midmorning, Ida came running out to the cutting shed and hollered for Sheldon.

"Sheldon, come quickly!"

Sheldon put down the fruit tray he was repairing and hurried to his mother.

"Mary Ellen is not doing well again," Ida gasped out. "She called and asked me to fetch you. You had better run see what she needs."

Sheldon ran to the house to see what he could find. Mary Ellen was breathing hard and complained of her arm and chest hurting. *Oh no,* thought Sheldon. *Sounds like a heart attack!*

Sheldon called Mary Ellen's parents and then grabbed the two youngest children and rushed them over to his parents' house. Then he ran back and cranked up his car. He waited impatiently for a truckload of workers to drive into the lane before he could pull out.

Sheldon drove swiftly through the streets of Modesto and out to the hospital in Ceres. At the hospital, he stopped next to the emergency room entrance. Mary Ellen was sweating profusely and moaning. A couple of nurses dressed in white scurried out to his car when he blew the horn. They brought a stretcher, and soon Mary Ellen was being wheeled into the emergency room.

A nurse monitored Mary Ellen and watched her heart beat.

"Mary Ellen, dear, can you hear me?" Sheldon spoke quietly to his wife. His stomach twisted to see her pale and unmoving. Bile rose in his throat at the thought of the pain she must be experiencing. *If only I could bear it for you, I would,* mourned the young husband. A blanket was drawn up over her shoulders. Her eyes blinked open for a moment and her hand twitched. She moaned.

"How is she doing?" Sheldon turned to the nurse.

"Not good, sir." She looked away.

Sheldon sat down and waited for the nurse to return. Mary Ellen's eyes were closed. The window blind was down and the room was dim. He could hear a nurse talking in the hallway. In another room nearby, a patient was complaining. The place was filled with that sterilized smell present in all hospitals. *Father, help Mary Ellen,* he prayed. *We had three successful births, but now this.*

Dr. James Woolsey stepped into the room.

"Sheldon, your wife is not well. We are doing all we can, but I don't have a lot of encouragement. We have started her on medications to prevent blood clotting around her heart. But with her heart defect, it is possible she won't make it. I want you to know that we will do all we can to save her." Dr. Woolsey looked down. "Maybe you should go get a few photos of your children and come back and tell her you need her. Encourage her. Maybe she will be awake later."

Glad to have something to do, Sheldon drove home, stopping by at his parents' house to let them know how serious Mary Ellen's condition was. He also called Joseph and Flossie to tell them Dr. Woolsey's news.

"Don't worry about the farming or the children," Walter said, coming to the house when he saw Sheldon arrive. "We have everything under control."

It was another warm day in Modesto as Sheldon walked to the house. Everything was quiet. The dishes had been washed and the kitchen and the living room were cleaned and organized with a note from Flossie on the table.

> *Don't worry about anything, Sheldon. We love you and are praying for you. ~Flossie*

Sheldon pulled out their photo albums and searched for some of Mary Ellen's favorite pictures of the children and the family. He fell to his knees in anguished prayer before heading back to the hospital.

When Sheldon walked into the room again where Mary Ellen was still lying, it seemed the nurse and doctor were more sober than they were earlier. They did not look up, but continued to watch the screens and monitor her heart.

"Is she better, Doctor?" Sheldon tried to keep the tremble from his voice.

"No sir. She is almost gone."

Sheldon's heart caught and he choked back a sob as he stumbled to Mary Ellen's side. He could not lose his wife! It was too soon. *Why, Lord?*

"Dear." Sheldon's voice trembled as he bent close. "I need you. Can you hear me? We need you!"

Mary Ellen's eyelids wrinkled as if she was trying to open them. Sheldon continued to talk to her. Finally, after spending an hour by her side, she began to respond. Her eyes opened. She observed the photos Sheldon held for her to see.

"Our family really needs you, Mary Ellen," he choked despite his determination to sound cheerful. "We love you."

Mary Ellen smiled faintly and fell asleep. Sheldon continued to hold her hand and pray. He lost track of time. Monitors hummed and lights blinked. *I wish it didn't have to smell like antiseptic all the time,* he thought angrily.

The door creaked open behind him. Light from the doorway spilled into the room and a shadow flickered across the bed. Someone moved close.

"Whatever you did, son, it worked," said Doctor Woolsey. "It looks as though she might be pulling through. Her heart's ticking better."

Oh, the relief! Sheldon came to the hospital once a day to be with Mary Ellen and read the Bible and pray together. Their parents and brothers and sisters also came to see her. Various ones of their church family stopped by to bring gifts and give encouragement.

Sheldon was overjoyed and thankful for the answered prayers and a recovering wife. Mary Ellen was now at home and resting. Two-year-old Becky snuggled up to her mother. Mark and Marilyn sat on the couch and looked at picture books.

Whatever life brings, I can always count on God to carry me through, Sheldon rejoiced. *The darkest night will always give way to dawn.* He stood up and went outside. It was dark except for a rising moon. The words of the Psalmist flashed through his mind. "Yea, though I walk through the valley of the shadow of death, I will fear no evil: for thou art with me."[2] *God, you will always be with me!* Sheldon raised his arm in grateful worship.

---

[2] Psalm 23:4

chapter ten
CHANGING TIMES

1951–1952

Sheldon watched as the Wood Colony folks crowded close to see the burial. Sheldon's grandmother Maggie Boyd Grover had passed away, leaving Grandpa Ira behind, somehow diminished and old. He couldn't help but think of all the good times they had experienced as a family at the home place on Shoemake with Grandma. As the grave slowly filled with rich Stanislaus soil, the members of the Modesto German Baptist Brethren Church slowly retreated. The sky was clear and the wind was still as tears dropped on smooth and wrinkled cheeks.

Since Mary Ellen was still recovering from her heart attack, she had stayed at home with Becky. Sheldon, along with Mark and Marilyn, attended the funeral service at the Modesto District church and then the burial at the Wood Colony Cemetery.

His mind began to cover the territory he had often explored since he was married. *How long would Mary Ellen be with him? She had a heart condition and there was no promise that she would live long. He still trusted that God would give her health, but what if...* His chest grew tight as he contemplated what all might happen yet. To say he was thankful that she had recovered from the heart attack would be a great understatement. He had read the statistics for those recovering from a heart attack and they were not good, especially not for women. He shook himself back to the present and held Mark and Marilyn closer.

The days following Grandma's funeral were tough ones for Grandpa and the family. Grandpa now lived alone, but Sheldon would regularly check to see how he was doing. It was convenient that Ira's house was between his grandson and his son Walter's.

"I am growing older," Ira said slowly. "Life brings changes whether you like it or not, but it is a blessing to trust in Him who does not change. I can't do as much as I could when I was younger and what I can do, I can't do very fast. But I can still do something and so I will do that." *What an inspiration,* Sheldon thought. *I wonder if I could adapt to a life-changing event as well as Grandpa.*

Mary Ellen was doing better and was now able to make meals and wash clothes. Jenny, the lady from Holland, also came and helped until Mary Ellen was fully recovered. Some days the young mother sat in her chair next to the lampstand and read Bible stories to the children or mended clothing. To her left was the crib in which little Becky slept. Mary Ellen was thankful that Sheldon could come in from the farm for meal times and that he was close by if there was ever an emergency. Her heart attack had brought an element of suspense to daily life.

For as long as Sheldon could remember, he had helped cultivate and harvest peaches on his father's and grandfather's adjacent properties. Before he had been drafted, they had rented the forty acres over on Woodland Avenue after Merven moved down to Hatch Road. The fruit harvested at the Woodland orchards was hauled to Walter's dry yard where it was cut, sulfured, and dried before being put into boxes for market.

Now they were caring for almond trees on another property. As usual,

Sheldon researched and studied the best ways to raise and cultivate these trees. He found literature about almond trees and talked with growers about their experiences with raising and harvesting nuts. During these years, the walnut orchard on the Ralph Landes property became available so Sheldon also farmed this. He and Ralph shared the profit each year.

Sheldon now began to research the possibility of purchasing a small tractor of his own. He stopped by the tractor dealership in Modesto one day to see what was available. The salesman showed him various models and gave him literature.

"All really nice models," said the salesman. "Never find any better than these slick tractors. Gone are the days of hitching horses and wagons and getting kicked when you ain't watching." He wrinkled his nose disdainfully. "Yep, you need to buy a tractor."

"Could you start up the John Deere MC and let me see how it runs?" asked Sheldon.

"No, sir. Not unless I know you're serious and not just lookin'." He grinned obnoxiously and jiggled the coins in his pocket. "You got any money or are you wastin' my time?"

"Well," said Sheldon calmly, keeping his ire under stern control, "I am looking for a tractor to buy for our orcharding but I guess I don't have to buy here." He smiled blandly.

"Oh now, don't get your dander up. Come over and I'll show you how this beauty runs. But you can't drive it."

After Sheldon came home that evening, he showed his wife the pamphlets the salesman had given him. He dropped the papers on the lampstand and picked up little Becky who had been crying.

"I'm not sure why she is fussing." Mary Ellen stirred the potatoes. "Maybe she's cutting another tooth." Little Becky quieted as Sheldon rocked her gently.

"What do you think, Mary Ellen? Shall we buy our own tractor to help with our orcharding and vineyard keeping, instead of using Pop's?" Sheldon moved to the table. "Pop's tractor is often in use when we need it for mowing hay or disking, and it would help to have another tractor for hauling fruit or nuts."

He recalled how, when he was a little boy, they used to do the orchard work with horses hitched to wagons with wide wooden wheels. This would certainly be an upgrade. He could even do some custom work with it. He jumped as his wife's voice brought him back to the present.

"Whatever you think, dear. You know what's best."

Sheldon enjoyed his wife's wonderful meal of fried potatoes and chicken, sliced tomatoes, and garden-fresh lettuce. After the meal, Sheldon helped Mary Ellen wash dishes. Then they sat together to look over the information about the tractors. Mark and Marilyn pushed close so they could see too.

When Sheldon purchased the John Deere MC crawler and brought it home, the children wanted to take a ride. First Mark and then Marilyn rode with Daddy on the new tractor. They waved excitedly to their mother who was holding Becky and watching the new machine.

One of the first things Sheldon used the tractor for was to dig a pit for burning trash and burying garbage. The children stood by and watched their father use a Fresno scraper to dig the hole in the sandy soil.

Sheldon and his son Mark on the John Deere MC crawler.

During the pruning and clean-up season, Sheldon also used the tractor to clean brush out of the orchard. It was also much easier now to harvest grapes in the vineyard since the new MC tractor was narrow enough to fit between the rows.

After school, Mark would come home to ride with Sheldon on the tractor or watch the peach cutters. Once Mark decided to help push the rail car loaded with fresh-cut peaches to the sulfur shed. A strong sulfur smell hung in the air, and his small nose wrinkled in spite of his determination to be a big helper. "I don't believe I'll push," he said. Artie Davison, Sheldon's uncle, was visiting from Kansas and helping for a day. Artie let out a mighty laugh and tipped his hat.

"Don't believe you'll push? Who's going to do it then, son?"

"Mark is learning that sulfur is for peaches and not for little boys to smell," said Sheldon with a tight grin.

In 1951, Sheldon heard that Clyde Miller was going to sell his property on Rumble Road near the church house. He and Mary Ellen knew the property well since the land had originally belonged to the Rumble family before it had been divided into lots and sold to various church members.

Clyde's one-and-a-half acre lot had a ranch-style house and three chicken houses. The house would be an upgrade for their growing family, and the chicken houses would provide additional income for them. This move would also allow Mary Ellen more privacy than what she had at the little house on Shoemake.

I guess I might have to swallow my words, Sheldon thought, remembering his sarcastic jabs at chicken farms and the accompanying odors. *Sometimes we need to do what needs to be done regardless of our feelings.* He could learn to deal with the squawking fowl, he supposed.

After Sheldon had discussed the terms for purchase with Clyde and gotten advice from a few brothers from church, he and Mary Ellen decided they would buy the place. It didn't take long to move their belongings to the new location with help from their families.

Sheldon and Mary Ellen worked together to organize the house with their furniture, household wares, and a few other possessions. Sheldon had help from his brothers-in-law to transport the larger appliances like the washing machine and refrigerator. Since it was harder for Mary Ellen to stand the summer heat after Becky's birth, Sheldon also bought and installed an air conditioner.

The children explored the property to discover all the hideouts and play spots while Mary Ellen planted flowerbeds and a garden. Sheldon planted walnut trees along the western side of the property.

Sheldon also continued his conversation with Clyde to determine the best way to raise broilers in the three chicken houses. He would purchase the chicks from the same company for now. Raising chickens would help Sheldon pay off the property and give the children something constructive to do as they grew older.

During these changing times Sheldon and Mary Ellen continued to teach their children truth through reading Bible stories and singing songs. Loving God and His church and providing for their family—these were the highest priorities for both Sheldon and Mary Ellen.

As far as Sheldon could tell, Mary Ellen was over her depression and heart problems. At least for the present, it seemed that way. But not he or anyone else could have guessed what they were going to experience next.

chapter eleven
"THOUGH HE SLAY ME"

1954

During the next couple of years, Sheldon and his father worked long, hard hours in the orchards, vineyards, and fields. Sheldon's dream had finally come true. He was a farmer.

Whether he was irrigating the orchards, sulfuring the vineyards, or cutting alfalfa hay, he threw himself into the work. He became toughened by the long hours of manual labor in the valley sunshine. He gained a reputation for being able to prune grapevines faster and better than many of his peers in Stanislaus County. The orchards he and his father cared for were kept very clean, properly sprayed, and well irrigated. Sheldon always had a market for his fruit and his wine grapes were in high demand.

His clean, orderly chicken houses were filled with peeping yellow balls of fluff, and he rose early to give them feed and water. He enjoyed watching a few tiny chicks run after a fly, then skid in bewilderment when the insect escaped their eager beaks.

"Keep your eye on the fly," he chuckled.

It had been three years since he had bought the property and poultry houses, and even though he had thought he would never have chickens, he not only had chickens now but was also raising them commercially. *Time limitations and other pragmatic factors can shape a man's destiny in a way his dreams never can,* he thought as he watched the chicks fight over another insect.

When Sheldon came into the house after the chores were completed, he found Mary Ellen making breakfast. The children waited at the little wooden table, rubbing their sleepy eyes. Sometimes one or two of the children would bounce into his lap as he sat down, and he held them close as the table was being set. Often he helped Mary Ellen put food on the table before they sat down together. The fatigue brought on by her heart problems and her occasional bouts of depression meant that Sheldon did more housework than many young husbands. *I guess I'd make a good single man,* he thought with a wry grin. *I know how to do most of the things that keep a home going.*

After a nourishing breakfast and a time of prayer with the family, Sheldon would start up his Chevy pickup and head to the home property to work with his father. Even though Walter was outspoken and a little unpolished, Sheldon enjoyed working with him. Pop, too, was a go-getter. Work got done when they put their minds to a job, and that was the way to make a good living and survive. The economy was slowly recovering from the aftermath of WWII, and a hardworking man could get on quite well if he was frugal and persistent.

In 1954, Sheldon was farming around eighty acres of peaches, apricots, and almonds, and forty acres of grapes; and then of course there were the three chicken houses filled with broilers on his own property. All year, on every day except Sunday, there was a whirlwind of activity and work throughout the whole day, and sometimes most of the night, too.

It was June and Sheldon had been irrigating all night on an uneven, forty-acre vineyard. Arriving home in the morning, he went to the broiler houses to feed the hungry fowl. Getting a wheelbarrow, he thrust it under the gravity flow bin outside to fill it with grain. The chickens flapped their wings and squawked with delight as Sheldon gave them grain. The air became dusty as the excited broilers scurried for their food. He sneezed. The litter and dust tickled his nose.

After the chores were finished, he walked tiredly to the house and stripped off his overalls, hanging them in the entry way. He got a whiff of crisp bacon and could hear eggs bubbling and sizzling as they fried in hot oil.

Sheldon washed his hands at the deep sink and then stepped into the kitchen. Mary Ellen was at the stove preparing breakfast. She was humming a tune as she worked.

"You look tired," she said sympathetically. "You have been working so hard. Did you work all night?"

"Yes dear, I was trying to get the irrigation finished." The bacon smell was making him ravenous. Sheldon sighed. "You're a wonderful wife, Mary Ellen."

"Hi, Daddy." Mark slid into his place at the table. Six-year-old Marilyn led little Becky, who was four, over to the table. Becky's blond curls bounced as she climbed onto Sheldon's lap. Marilyn stood beside his chair, her blue eyes looking up at him with admiration.

After enjoying a warm breakfast and kneeling in prayer with the family, Sheldon donned his overalls once again. He cranked up the Chevy pickup and drove back over to Woodland Avenue to finish the irrigating.

He whistled as he drove along meditating on the blessings and goodness of God. He was exactly where he wanted to be. His heart swelled in worship and his lips broke forth in song. He knew there was no promise it would always be this way, but now was now and it was good.

After the irrigating was finished, he drove back to the home place to complete the disking. *The tractor sure makes this job much easier*, he thought as he jumped onto the seat. His back and neck ached from the long sleepless night. *Surely I can make it until this evening*, he thought. A trickle of pain ran down his spine as the tractor jolted over a tough-looking root. He leaned over and grabbed a tall weed and jerked it out as he passed.

As Sheldon disked, he was almost too tired to enjoy the great outdoors he had loved so much ever since childhood. Native Indians had walked across this land for hundreds and maybe thousands of years. In the past two hundred years, the nationals had either been killed or died of infectious disease brought to the valley by the Spanish and European settlers. Now the land was cleared and he was bumping along on a tractor, disking the soil to keep down the weeds that irrigation had encouraged.

Sheldon scanned the skies. This was dry season. There was not a cloud in the skies except for the small one created by his disc. He could do without the dust but he supposed it was about the only disadvantage of living in the beautiful San Joaquin Valley.

Later in the afternoon, Sheldon parked the John Deere crawler in the barn and closed the doors. His father was tightening up the ladders they would use in harvest.

"How's it going, Sheldon?" Walter's brisk voice echoed across the barn. "Get it all disked or were you too tired of bouncing to finish?" He hung the hammer back on its peg.

"I'm really tired. Didn't sleep last night because I was irrigating." Sheldon lowered himself down gingerly on a hay bale. "I'm more sore than normal and my back is hurting."

"Go see the chiropractor for a treatment. That's my suggestion."

When Sheldon arrived home and walked to the house, he tripped on the doorstep and almost fell. The children watched, open-mouthed, not sure whether to be alarmed or amused at the sight of their daddy tripping the way they did sometimes. Sheldon reassured the little ones with a smile, and related to Mary Ellen how his day went and how tired and sore he was.

"Pop suggested I go to Dr. DeBoard for a treatment," he said wearily.

"I will take you," said Mary Ellen. "We need to get you feeling better. Let me help you bathe and dress and I'll call Mama. We can drop the children off at my parents on the way."

Soon the family was dressed and ready to leave. The children piled into their tan Ford station wagon, talking excitedly about going to Grandpa and Grandma's place. Mary Ellen helped Sheldon out to the car and into the passenger's seat. After a few minutes of bouncing along Rumble Road, they arrived at Grandpa Rumble's house where they left the children. Soon Mary Ellen and Sheldon arrived at the chiropractor's office.

After the treatment, Dr. DeBoard said, "Go home and get some rest, Sheldon. It looks like your body is tired out."

By the time they had picked up the children and arrived back home, the sun was hanging low in the western sky.

"Maybe the children and I can help you with the chores this evening?" suggested Mary Ellen.

"Yes," the children chorused. "Let's do it together!"

The family worked together to feed and water the eager chickens. Sheldon let the cracked grain slide through his fingers as he watched the fowl scurry to eat. He wasn't enjoying this like he usually did. He leaned against the wall for a moment.

That night Sheldon did not sleep well. His body continued to ache. *I didn't work any harder than other times.* He shifted uncomfortably in bed, trying yet another position. If he didn't feel better in the morning, he would go see Dr. Battle, he decided. Something more must be wrong. Surely it wasn't another case of poliomyelitis. He had heard there were at least seventy-five cases of polio in the latest outbreak that was now spreading through Stanislaus County. He was stronger than that. He just overdid it this time. He would try to take it easier and not push so hard to finish a job.

The next morning Mary Ellen had to help Sheldon prepare himself for a visit to the doctor. Sheldon first called Dr. Battle to see if it would be okay to come to his house.

"Come on over," he said. "We can at least talk."

"Working yourself to death, are you?" said Dr. Battle when Sheldon came in.

Sheldon explained what he had been doing and his sleep deficiency. "I didn't sleep Friday night at all since I was out irrigating. Last night I didn't sleep well either."

"You look as if you need rest, that's for sure," Dr. Batttle commented. "You need to come back tomorrow, and I will take a spinal tap to do some testing. It may be poliomyelitis."

As they drove home, Sheldon hoped that by taking time out to rest he would soon feel better. He hoped Dr. Battle was wrong about the polio. He didn't have time for that. This was the Lord's Day, so he would rest and maybe he would be doing better tomorrow. The sunlight washed over him as they turned the corner onto Rumble Road. The wind tousled his hair and calmed his nerves. As they pulled off Rumble Road into their driveway, he noted the improvements they had made since the purchase of the property. *The pine trees have put on some height in the two years we're here,* he thought with satisfaction, *and Mary Ellen's flower beds sure help to brighten the place up. But there are more improvements to be made.*

Monday morning, after a breakfast together and prayer, Mary Ellen and Sheldon decided to drop the children off at Grandpa Rumble's place on Dale Road and then go to Dr. Battle's office in Ceres. Mary Ellen squeezed Sheldon's hand reassuringly.

"Maybe it's not what we think," she said. "Maybe it's something else and you will be all right."

But Dr. Battle's tests confirmed his diagnosis. Sheldon had contracted the polio virus. There was nothing they could do but let it run its course, the doctor said. He recommended that Sheldon go immediately to the isolation ward at the hospital in downtown Modesto. "They should be able to at least make you comfortable and watch your condition as it progresses. But I'm afraid they are limited in what they can do," he said sadly.

In stunned silence, Mary Ellen and Sheldon paid the receptionist and left the office. The morning sun teased an aroma from the marigolds lining the sidewalks and a gentle wind tossed the blue gum tops. A Studebaker hummed along the street and a Pacific Southern train loaded with coal rumbled slowly through town along I-99. A teenage girl on a single speed bicycle stopped on the sidewalk and adjusted the pack on her back. Life was continuing on like normal—for everyone but this young couple.

The walk to the car was painful and Sheldon was beginning to have difficulty breathing. "I can take you wherever you want to go," said Mary Ellen worriedly. "I don't have to take you to the hospital." She started the car.

"I don't care." Sheldon lay back with a groan. "We should pray."

After prayer they decided to go to the hospital as the doctor had recommended. *What else was there to do?* Mary Ellen thought desperately. Two years ago she was the one in the hospital, and now it was Sheldon.

At the county hospital Sheldon could hardly get out of the car. Beginning to cry softly, Mary Ellen helped steady him as he stumbled into the reception area. His feet were like lumps of lead attached to unfeeling lengths of tissue. His body didn't obey him anymore.

"What are you here for?" the receptionist asked. She scribbled on the paper sheet on her clipboard.

After Sheldon was admitted, they took him in a wheelchair to the south wing on the first floor. He was helped into bed and then he lay still. The pain surged through his body and took away his breath. Light hurt his eyes, so he squeezed them shut. An hour passed. Then two. A doctor came into the room for a minute to look at Sheldon and then turned and left.

"I need to go care for the children, dear," said Mary Ellen softly, sitting on the edge of the bed and smoothing back his disheveled hair. "I'll be back as soon as I can."

My God, my God. Why hast thou forsaken me? Sheldon's heart heaved in desperation as he tried to move. He could not feel his right leg. He strained to move it, but nothing happened. *Oh God, what is happening? My God, oh God, help me.*

Sheldon's worsening condition was monitored by the hospital staff. When he was completely paralyzed from the neck down, they moved him to a rocking bed. This hospital bed rocked Sheldon as if he were lying on a seesaw; head up and feet down, then feet up and head down. Gravity helped him breathe. As his feet went down, his internal organs moved toward his feet and his lungs expanded. When his head went down, the organs moved toward his head and pushed the air out of his lungs. An active, wiry man in the full strength of his life, he was unable to breathe on his own.

The days and nights blurred together as Sheldon's body fought to survive the acute stage of the active paralytic poliomyelitis virus. Sheldon wavered between life and death.

Since the cause and transmission of polio was not known at that time, no children and few adults were allowed into the hospital. Mary Ellen took the children to the hospital to the south wing where there was a small window through which they could see their father. Eight-year-old Mark could stretch and see into the room where his father lay strapped to the rocking bed. Mary Ellen lifted Marilyn and Becky so they too could see Daddy.

Over and over, Mary Ellen found herself pleading to God for her husband. The children, too, reminded Mama to pray for Daddy. They knelt together at home and prayed for his life and healing. Their many prayers ascended to make one long continuous cry to God to save their daddy and husband.

Walter and Ida Grover came by frequently to check on Mary Ellen and the children. Joseph and Flossie Rumble, who lived only a few blocks away, also came over to help out. The German Baptist church folks made sure that Mary Ellen and the children had what they needed and helped with chores and orcharding.

"How are you doing, Mary Ellen?" Flossie's arm circled her daughter's frail shoulders. "Are you getting enough rest?"

"Oh, Mother," sighed Mary Ellen, tears filling her eyes. "It is very hard. I don't know how much more of this I can handle. I could hardly manage before Sheldon became ill."

Mother and daughter held each other and wept. Life was difficult enough with the strain of motherhood and making a living, not to mention having a hurting and handicapped husband.

"God will see us through, Mary Ellen. He is good." Their tears subsided as their embrace relaxed. Mary Ellen brushed away a few lingering tears.

In the hospital, Sheldon began to slowly improve and after a couple of weeks could breathe on his own again. His body, though it had built immunity against the polio virus, was now left paralyzed.

Paralyzed. Would he ever be able to move again? Sheldon stared drearily at the ceiling and thought about his passion for worship and attending church functions. Would this ever be possible again? He had always attended the planned activities at church with a deep inner anticipation and joy, knowing that true fellowship with God came through close fellowship with his brothers and sisters in the church.

And what about his aim to pay off his mortgage and debts? *I wanted to get ahead in life, and I was finally beginning to get there!* He knew what being poor was and dreamed of having plenty; enough to please Mary Ellen and plenty to give away. Now he might not even be able to provide food and clothing, basic needs for his family. He didn't need to be rich but he didn't want to be dependent on others either. Some of the stigma had been erased when he got his queen—Mary Ellen.

Sheldon tossed his head from side to side on the hot pillow, trying to release his mounting frustration. He wanted to move, to change positions in this miserable bed. Only his upper torso moved a little. *Like a baby*, he thought bitterly. *I am not much better now than a newborn.* He cringed—he was definitely dependent on others now. This was awful. *I'm a man!* He wanted to scream the words to an uncaring world. A sob shook his upper body and reverberated all the way down to his soul.

Mary Ellen came nearly every day to bring Sheldon a little gift from the children or a treat from one of the church families. She took time to read the Scriptures to him and pray with him. Sheldon's spirit was lifted when his dear wife came and visited him. She was such a blessing to him that he could not imagine living without her.

One day, after a few weeks had passed, the doctor came into Sheldon's room. He sat beside him and scooted his chair close. With his left hand, he steadied his clipboard against his protruding stomach while he jotted down a few notes. His thinning hair seemed almost too black against his pale skin. He tapped his forehead with his pencil, then turned to see Sheldon eyeing him.

"It looks as if it's time to start therapy," he said briskly but not unkindly. "You have been able to move your upper body some, it appears on the record. You are actually lucky to be alive. There are others who were as bad off as you were who are now six feet under. Anyway, we will need to fuse your spine so you can sit up because you will never be able to sit up by yourself.

"The next step is for a nurse to take you to the therapy department each day," he continued, unaware or uncaring of the impact his words were having on his listener, pinned helplessly in the bed. "It's essential that we help you reactivate the muscles that were atrophied due to the nerve damage. We need to get you back out into your orchards somehow." He brought up his arm and coughed in his sleeve. "You're a working man." His face, which had turned red from the cough, returned to its original paleness.

After the doctor strode out the door, Sheldon thought about the doctor's words. He hoped that somehow he could get out of bed and try to regain the use of his limbs. Maybe there was some hope hidden in the doctor's words. Maybe he would walk again. Sheldon's brow wrinkled in an effort to push away the doctor's words, *". . . you'll never be able to sit up by yourself."* He would now need to go through therapy each day to stimulate the use of the atrophied muscles and limp joints. There was no promise that he would regain anything, but he was hopeful and determined.

As Sheldon lay flat on his back, motionless, he had a lot of time to think about the future and what he would do once he got better. If only he could hurry up his improvement and start therapy to get back in shape. At least he was still living and would be able to provide for Mary Ellen and the children. He missed his little ones. He would need to hang in there. He would soon be out of this prison and back into the fields and orchards. He could already smell the blossoms and feel the wind in his hair.

chapter twelve
MORE PRECIOUS THAN GOLD

1954

During the 1940s and 1950s, polio swept like wildfire around the globe, ravaging millions. In many countries, it was killing or paralyzing more than five hundred thousand people each year. Other victims were so paralyzed they could no longer breathe on their own, so iron lungs, the mechanical ventilators, kept them alive. The "lucky" few that made it through the horrible ordeal had to walk on crutches the remainder of their lives. In some parts of the world, the handicapped were simply put out of their misery.

In 1947, the University of Pittsburgh recruited Jonas Salk to develop a virus program at Pitt. The efforts of the university's polio research team ended in a controlled field trial, the largest in history.[1]

Around two million children across the United States, as well as some from Canada, were involved in this field trial, which was arranged by the

---

[1] http://www.225.pitt.edu/story/ending-polio%27s-reign-terror

National Foundation for Infantile Paralysis, or March of Dimes. At the trial's successful conclusion, the U.S. government approved the vaccine for the public in April of 1955, very soon after Sheldon had contracted polio.

Back on the farm Walter Grover was taking charge and organizing some of the men from church to continue Sheldon's orcharding and vineyard keeping. A few of them also helped Mary Ellen and the children care for the laying hens. Mary Ellen's mother and sisters came by whenever they could to drop off a meal or help with the children. Sometimes they would take the children home with them to mind them and give them an opportunity to play with their cousins.

Sheldon's therapist, Mr. Harley, came each day to take him for his exercises. He was a tough-looking man with a reddish brown beard and a bald head. He always wore a tie. "My wife likes it," he said. And his shoes? Always black and spotlessly clean. But his eyes were what impressed Sheldon. They glimmered with compassion, and Sheldon warmed to him immediately.

"I think I can help you," said Mr. Harley as he stroked his beard. He sat so close to the edge of his chair it appeared he might fall off at any given moment.

"I wouldn't let the doctors fuse your spine for sure because that would definitely limit your ability long term. With lots of exercise and therapy, I can see you walking again, and," he shrugged his shoulders with a smile, "maybe even running."

A warm breeze wafted in through the open window, bringing with it the smell of distant almond blossoms, which inflamed Sheldon's heart with the desire to walk again. He saw himself once again leading his son or daughter by the hand, picking peaches in the orchard, or climbing Half Dome. The adrenaline rush numbed his pain for a moment.

"Whatever you say, sir," he said. "I'm willing to try it. I'll do everything I can to be able to walk again."

Mr. Harley rubbed his left eyebrow with the back of his hand. "But I'm going to be realistic with you, sir," he said. "It's going to be a long, hard climb. But I do want you to know that I'll be right beside you every step of the way."

A week passed and then another as Sheldon worked hard at the exercises recommended by Mr. Harley. Each morning Sheldon was assisted in rising and dressing for the day. After he was dressed, he spent quiet time in prayer before his breakfast. *Oh God, give me strength,* he prayed. *I can't do this alone. I need your help.*

Mr. Harley showed up every day at Sheldon's room on the dime. Sheldon was wheeled to the therapy room in the basement, where he followed Mr. Harley's instructions to work on developing his muscles again. The therapist's tie swung like a pendulum as he demonstrated how to exercise.

Sheldon set his jaw, grimly determined to do his utmost to get back in shape.

"Don't give up," the therapist would say. "Keep trying. You can do it! See, your right hand is now beginning to work. Good job!"

One of Sheldon's workouts included an exercise wheel that was donated to the polio therapy ward. This large wheel looked like an upright Ferris wheel and was mounted on the brick wall in the hospital basement. Sheldon would grasp the handle on the wheel and turn it around and around to exercise his upper body. Some of this ongoing treatment was made possible through March of Dimes donations.

There were also braces Sheldon used as he attempted to walk. The braces would be strapped to his legs, and he would take a walker and try to shuffle around to exercise the atrophied muscles. The pain in his legs and back was excruciating.

"I understand," said Mr. Harley, wincing. "It probably almost takes your breath away, but don't give up yet. Here, take a drink of water."

He handed Sheldon a cool glass of water and pulled out his hanky to wipe his forehead. He checked his watch.

"It's about time for my next patient," he remarked. The weary sufferer felt relief at the idea of stopping, but dismay at the thought of not continuing to progress with the therapist's aid.

After a few months passed, Sheldon's brother Merven asked the doctors and therapists to allow Sheldon to go home to be with his family. He assured the doctors that he would bring him back once a day as long as he needed more therapy.

"If I can't come in for some reason, I will find someone else to bring Sheldon," he promised. "This way he can at least be at home with his family."

Returning home was a milestone for Sheldon in his hopeful journey to recovery. The ride may have been painful, but a glimmer of light was beginning to shine at the end of the seemingly endless tunnel. Not just because he was almost home, but also because this was the start of another era for him. It would be another upward climb, one that had already started. It would be a slow climb, but a climb nonetheless.

Every weekday, Sheldon was carried to a waiting vehicle and then transported to the hospital for treatments. For the first couple of weeks the driver had to tie Sheldon to the seat to keep him from falling over. But eventually his muscles gained strength and he could sit upright without falling against the dash or the door.

Sheldon continued his exercises at home with help from Mary Ellen or eight-year-old Mark. He would put on his leg braces and position his walker to practice using his legs. He moaned with pain, sweat pouring off his face. It was just so hard to walk. But with determination, he would get up and try to get his stiffened muscles to work loose.

"Do you have to keep trying to walk if it is so painful?" asked Mark. He helped Sheldon strap the braces for the daily trial. He wished his daddy could just be healed. It would be so much easier.

"I suppose if I want to walk again, I will need to ignore the pain and keep trying." Sheldon grimaced as he tried to stand.

After several months of returning to the hospital for therapy, the therapist said, "Mr. Grover, you need to make a decision. Either you must spend all your waking hours in therapy, or be in a wheelchair for the rest of your life."

Mr. Harley blushed a shade pinker and tried to swallow as Sheldon stared at him with unblinking eyes.

"I don't have to think about it, sir. I already know my answer. I have a wife and three children at home, so somehow I have got to make a living from my wheelchair. I don't know how . . . but I can't make a living if I spend all my time on myself, just trying to walk."

"As you please," Mr. Harley shrugged and twitched his tie into place.

Although Sheldon's mind was exploring the possibilities of increased income for his family, he continued to go for therapy each week. He now went a couple of days a week to see Mrs. Laura Nichols, a therapist in a nearby town of Riverbank, about fifteen minutes from Modesto. Often Don Beachler took Sheldon to Mrs. Nichols, though sometimes Mary Ellen took him in the family car. On such occasions they often stopped to refuel at the filling station in Riverbank since gas was only twenty-four cents a gallon there.

"We will need to make every move count," reminded Sheldon. "We are going to Riverbank anyway, so why not get gas where it's cheapest?"

Sheldon missed the fruit and nut harvests as the summer and autumn passed. The harvest had ended, and he was not improving as fast as he dreamed he would. His dream of working in the orchards had passed with the hot summer and autumn winds. His mind went to the Scriptures. *God is working in me to prepare my soul for the return of my Savior . . . that the trial of your faith, being much more precious than of gold that perishes, though it be tried with fire, might be found unto praise and honor and glory at the appearing of Jesus Christ.*[2] *God help me*, he thought. He gritted his teeth. He must continue to push harder and think smarter.

---

[2] 1 Peter 1:7

chapter thirteen
"I CAN DO ALL THINGS"

1955

Sheldon wrestled with the idea of not going out to the orchards again. Not ever again. That was a very tough thought. All those dreams had been stripped out of his life like polio had stripped the sheath off his nerves. He might not have feeling in his body anymore, but he had lots of feelings in his heart. Deep feelings. Gloomy feelings. Tough feelings.

At first, Sheldon could hardly make his wheelchair go through his chicken houses since the litter and manure would gum up on his wheels. But he was determined. He had to check the feeders and the water and make sure everything was working properly. He would go down to the end and come back, and then again. He did this through all three chicken houses until he was exhausted. The fryers squawked and jumped and flapped their wings as he passed. Their excitement stirred more dust into the air.

How God, could you let this happen? Thoughts and emotions like the smothering dust nearly suffocated him. And the stigma of being handicapped—how could he deal with it?

His mind groped for hope and reassurance. He couldn't wallow in self-pity. Would not the Judge of all the earth do right? He never made a mistake in His plans.

As Sheldon tried to relax, his mind traveled back to the hospital where he had met Randy. Randy had also been a polio victim and had lain beside Sheldon during those critical months. Randy had regained some strength but was also confined to a wheelchair and needed care. But after he returned home, his wife had stuck him into a back bedroom and told him to stay there. She was afraid he would slip and fall or trip and break her beautiful china or other knickknacks in the house. With all the throw rugs over the hardwood floors, it was hard to get around with a wheelchair anyway. "So," she said, "the best thing is just to stay in your room." More recently, Sheldon had heard that Randy lost hope and died after his wife divorced him.

Mary Ellen not only helped Sheldon with adjustments indoors but also helped as she could in little ways outside too. After a tough few hours in the chicken houses, Sheldon would wheel back to the house with chicken manure stuck on his wheels and hands. He would call to Mary Ellen, who came as soon as she could to hose down his wheelchair and help him get clean before he went inside.

There has got to be a way to generate more profit. Sheldon's thoughts groped frantically for ideas. The children were growing and it was simply going to require more money to feed and clothe the family. Even though they cut corners and made use of everything they had, it still took more. Mary Ellen sewed little coats for the children and mended their clothing to make things last longer. Leftovers were reheated and eaten. Any product that could be recycled was saved. It may not have been the Great Depression, but a dearth had come back to trouble them.

Sheldon explored the possibilities of changing from broilers to layers for more income. After some direction and advice from church friends, it was decided to renovate the chicken houses so cages could be put in for the laying hens. Walter and some of the men from church helped with the conversion.

They installed hanging wire cages with a bottom that sloped toward the aisle so the eggs would roll down to the edge.

Before long the layers arrived, were put into the cages, and were finally laying eggs. Sheldon and the children collected, cleaned, and crated eggs every day except Sunday. Before and after school, the children helped with the work. The children did most of the cleaning since Sheldon's left hand didn't work well.

Sheldon normally arose early to prepare for the day and Mary Ellen helped him when she could. He got into his wheelchair and wheeled himself outside and to the chicken houses. What he used to do with ease and without thought now took prayer and much effort. His 34-year-old mind was still young and creative, but his body was twisted, crippled, and filled with pain.

As he wheeled himself out of the house, sometimes Marilyn or Becky went with him. Other times he was the first one out in the chicken houses since he often rose early in the morning to prepare for the day and to spend time in worship. Prayer was becoming an integral part of everything he did. As he wheeled back and forth doing the chores, pain coursed through his arms and neck. Sheldon gritted his teeth and repeated his favorite verse in his mind. *I can do all things through Christ which strengtheneth me.*[1] Then he took a deep breath and pushed himself to the next cage to gather eggs. Now that the layers had replaced the fryers, the concrete floors between the cages were bare instead of being covered with litter. This made it easier and cleaner and gave Sheldon increased mobility in his work.

After the eggs had been collected and cleaned, the children placed them into egg flats and cases for sale in the cold room. Sometimes local customers would come and buy a few dozen in egg cartons, but most of them were collected each week by the company with whom they had a contract.

About the time the chicken houses were altered, Sheldon decided he needed a better way to do his chores. After some research, he decided to buy an electric cart and convert it to drive through the chicken houses to feed the chickens or to gather eggs. At Woody Poultry Supply in Livingston, California,

---

[1] Philippians 4:13

he found a standard electric cart made for working in laying hen operations. He then asked his good friend Howard Flory, a genius at inventing, to add a seat to the cart that could be raised and lowered. Howard found a part from an airplane's landing gear, called an electric-powered ram, to raise and lower the seat. In this way, Sheldon could lower the seat down to the height of his wheelchair, making it possible for him to slide onto, or off of, the new electric cart. He could then raise it up to feed chickens or gather eggs. He could also lower it all the way down to work in his garden.

Sheldon would charge the batteries on the cart overnight and then have enough power during the day to drive around to do his chores. He would take his baskets or trays and fill them with eggs and stack them on his cart. It was much easier and more convenient than driving his wheelchair. There was also a metal feed bin that could be scooted onto the cart and filled with feed from the gravity flow bin outside the first house.

After an exhausting day of hard work, Sheldon was dragging with fatigue but still enjoyed the time with the family around the table. The children talked about the day at school, and Mary Ellen shared with Sheldon tidbits of news she had heard from her mother or other friends she had spoken with that day.

The egg cart, a standard electric cart made for working in layer operations.

"Dad just got back from New York City this morning," said Mary Ellen, turning from the potatoes and ham she was stirring. "The broker had called and told him that every train-car load of watermelons that arrived was spoiled and he couldn't pay."

"So he went and checked them out?" Sheldon grinned. "Sounds like him."

"Yes. Mom said that he

didn't tell the broker he was coming. Just walked in and asked to see the melons. They were all fine. None were spoiled."

"He got his money?"

"Yes."

Not just anyone would have made the trip clear across the country to verify the claim. But Joseph Rumble was a businessman and he had become successful in the trade for a reason.

Sheldon thought about *his* progress in becoming fruitful in business. Just when he had been at his prime, he had been crushed. It didn't seem fair. He now would have to be innovative simply to put bread on the table.

"I just wiggled my big toe on my right foot," he said suddenly.

"I want to see it," squealed Becky. The children scooted back their chairs and ran around the table. Sheldon rolled back his wheelchair and tried to show them, but to no avail. The toe wouldn't wiggle again, try as he would. They all watched intently as Sheldon tried several more times.

"Oh well," sighed Mary Ellen, "at least there is improvement." She picked up the kettle of left-over potatoes and ham and set them back onto the counter. The children giggled about the big toe that wouldn't wiggle. Sheldon looked at his youngsters with a tight grin.

His family was an important factor in his journey to healing. He would be forever indebted to Mary Ellen for her patience with him. And the children helped with the healing process. Wheelchair or not, it was life and things had become abruptly normal for them. They accepted and loved their father without reservation or shame; no looking down their noses or sideways pitying glances. No wonder Jesus said that except we become as little children, we will not enter the kingdom of heaven.

And now there would be a fourth child. The pregnancy had come as a surprise and had caused Mary Ellen much anxiety at first, thinking of what could happen. She had so much to do already with a handicapped husband. And it was only four years since she had nearly died of an all-but-fatal heart attack. Now it was May, and the baby was due in less than seven weeks.

/ /

After the evening meal, Sheldon rested in his chair while Mary Ellen and the children washed dishes and cleaned the kitchen. Because he liked to read and research new or updated methods in almost any field, he subscribed for literature and magazines to study. One of his greatest passions was the Second Coming of Jesus and end-time events, and that passion had grown over the past year. "Perhaps today" became his watchword as he worked or sat praying and studying the Scriptures.

Because the heat bothered her, Mary Ellen could not help much with the outdoor chores, but she did all she could indoors to make life easier for Sheldon. She kept the house in order, got rid of all the throw rugs on the floors, washed clothes, made meals, and helped Sheldon bathe and dress when he needed help.

For bathing, Sheldon had a bar installed at hand height over the bathtub. The men from church had built onto the bathroom and installed a bathtub for him after he had been inflicted with polio. Now by using the smooth board he had made, he slid from his wheelchair to the edge of the bathtub. With his stronger right arm, he could lift his legs in and then lower himself down into the water.

Sometimes Mary Ellen had to cry as she watched Sheldon struggle to dress himself or try to complete a job that just a year or two ago would have been easy. Sometimes no tears came as her heart wrenched within her. She would go to his rescue as often as she could, but sometimes she was just too tired to get up and help.

Why did they need to be inflicted with more pain and difficulty? Mary Ellen wiped her eyes. There was enough stress with her problems. And now she was heavy with child. "O God, help me," she murmured. "Help me be thankful."

Now that Mary Ellen was nearing her due date, it took more time for her and Sheldon to complete daily duties. But with the children's help, they managed to get by and sometimes her mother or siblings came to help. More than ever, they were grateful for the community and the brotherhood.

On July 2, 1955, a second son, Harold, was born to Sheldon and Mary Ellen. He was born without any major complications, for which everyone was thankful. *A beautiful little boy*, thought Sheldon as he held his newborn son. *O Father, help me teach him from your Word. May he be a strong, healthy son. A real warrior.*

Family members came to help with the meals and chores, and Sheldon kept on doing all he could even though he was often in pain. Early in the morning, he would wake up before the sun rose and he would just lie there praying. He could hear a few vehicles going past their house. A mockingbird joined the dawn chorus.

I can do all things through Christ which strengtheneth me. Sheldon's favorite verse had become a special prayer. *O Father, before the mountains were brought forth, or ever thou hadst formed the earth and the world, even from everlasting to everlasting, thou art God.*[2]

Sometimes as Sheldon lay in the early morning darkness, Harold would whimper and cry. Since Sheldon was practically powerless to get up and help him, Mary Ellen would wake up, roll over, and get out of bed to see what he needed. Sometimes Harold needed to be changed, other times he was hungry, and sometimes he just needed the blanket tucked under his chin and a reassuring kiss. No matter whether the need was urgent or simple, Sheldon lay helpless and watched while his frail wife took care of it.

Another day would unfold with Sheldon getting up and dressing to go out and work. It took him at least an hour to dress, and that was by doing it as fast as he could. If no one could help him with getting what he needed, he simply figured out a way to do it by himself.

Now and then Mary Ellen's father Joseph brought visitors to their house from the East. As a minister, he hosted many of these guests who wanted to meet Sheldon. They stopped by to hear Sheldon's story, to see his innovative ways of operating in spite of his limitations, and to encourage him to be faithful. Sheldon usually enjoyed these visits from family, locals, or Christian brothers and sisters from out-of-state, but sometimes he simply endured them.

---

[2] Psalm 90:2

"It's fine for people to stop by and visit," he grumbled later to Mary Ellen, "but why do they need to stay so long? I've got work to do, even if they are on vacation!"

Sometimes Sheldon would sit outside and enjoy nature. He would study or just sit and absorb the sun for a few minutes before wheeling on to do some physical labor.

"Becky," called Sheldon as he wheeled out into the sunlight for a few minutes during the day. "Can you bring my Bible to me? It's on my stand."

It was in the afternoon and the sun was still high in the sky, but a few trees gave a little shade. Soon Becky came bouncing back with the big black Bible held precariously in her little hands. Sheldon opened his Bible and read. "Wherefore seeing we also are compassed about with so great a cloud of witnesses, let us lay aside every weight, and the sin which doth so easily beset us, and let us run with patience the race that is set before us, Looking unto Jesus the author and finisher of our faith; who for the joy that was set before him endured the cross."[3] A dry breeze kicked up a fine dust, the weeds along the drive rustled, and the almond trees whispered nature's secrets.

Sheldon eyes grew moist. Longing tugged at his heart till he could hardly bear it. *I won't be running any more physical races or climbing Half Dome or fishing Rock Creek. My legs won't carry me for that. But this race set before me . . . I can run this one. And I can run it with patience—or endurance, as the word actually means.*

The breeze turned a page of his Bible as Sheldon contemplated the changes in his life. A mosquito whined around his head and he swatted at it weakly with his good hand. Mark came tearing into the driveway on his bicycle, having completed an errand for his mother. Marilyn and Becky sat on the steps playing with a baby kitten. Sheldon could hear Mary Ellen singing somewhere. *Even though there are some dark threads in the fabric of life,* he thought, *by God's grace, I will endure and I will win.*

---

[3] Hebrews 12:1, 2

chapter fourteen
ANOTHER OBSTACLE CONQUERED

1956

Sheldon wheeled to the living room after lunch to rest a few minutes before going back to work. It had been two years since the polio epidemic and his life was trying to find an even keel. With constant prayer to his heavenly Father, much help from his wife and children, and continued support from his church family, he was able to endure the pain of recovery.

He prayed constantly for strength and wisdom. Before he could get out of bed, he had to pray. He would also quote his theme verse: "I can do all things through Christ which strengthens me." Truly, prayer came first with Sheldon.

A couple of times a week, one of the church brothers took him for his therapy treatments. Pop was in and out almost every day to see if anything needed to be done or to drop off some fresh fruit he had picked. Often the brothers or sisters from church stopped in to help with fixing something or just to chat and see how things were going.

Sheldon watched as Mary Ellen rocked Harold and sang a lullaby. The day was warm but indoors it was cool. Mary Ellen had remarked more than once how grateful she was that he had installed an air conditioner for her when they had moved to the house on Rumble Road. The late summer days were warm and draining, but the cool air from the humming machine was refreshing.

His heart warmed as he thought of Mary Ellen's constant love and care for him. Why had he ever contemplated not marrying her? Now *he* needed care. He was learning a valuable lesson through his experiences. Never try to play God. Let God be God and learn to trust and follow Him.

He finally gave up his passion for going back to orcharding and was now thinking about ways to overcome the obstacles before him. He still wanted to work with plants and trees. Raising a garden was helping to satisfy his love of working with plants. He also wanted to work with flowers and trees. Surely he could think of something in that department.

One thing he really wanted to do again was drive a car. This would make him less dependent on others and allow him to travel, at least locally. Mary Ellen was not completely comfortable driving and sometimes it made Sheldon a little nervous when she drove. Once as they were returning from Mrs. Nichols, the therapist, they had a close call. They were leaving the gas station in Riverbank and Mary Ellen hadn't seen a motorcycle coming. Sheldon had hollered and she had hit the brakes just in time. The cruiser had also swerved to miss them.

"All's well that ends well," he croaked as he wiped a few beads of sweat from his forehead. "It could have happened to anyone," he comforted Mary Ellen.

Ever since he was back home from the hospital, he had contemplated how he could drive again. Maybe in his condition, he wouldn't be much safer than Mary Ellen. He forced a chuckle.

Maybe our mechanic, Ira Denlinger, could redesign something in our car so that I can drive it again, thought Sheldon as he rolled his wheelchair through the kitchen toward the back porch. He decided to contact Ira that very evening. Sheldon's natural impatience still surged, trapped inside a body that didn't respond.

The afternoon passed by slowly as Sheldon worked in the chicken houses. The work was hot and dusty but at least he could work. He continued to pray for strength to keep gathering eggs and feeding the chickens. As he drove his motorized cart back and forth, he pondered the best way to design his car so he could drive it. *Perhaps a hand brake could be installed,* he thought. *And we could somehow move the accelerator so I could use my left foot for that.* The polio had left his right leg and left arm most affected with weakness. Brother Ira probably would have ideas how to customize their Ford station wagon for handicapped drivers.

As usual, by mid-afternoon the schoolchildren had arrived at home. Following a light snack, they came running out to help clean and box eggs.

"Hi, Mark and Marilyn! How was school?" Sheldon loved to see his youngsters help with the chores. He was amazed at how well they did.

Soon Mark and Marilyn were putting the eggs through the egg washer, their childish chatter providing a musical background. Water sprayed onto the eggs and little brushes cleaned them. The eggs were then rolled under a light to show up blood spots. Any defective eggs were set aside as seconds and sold to local customers for a discounted price.

Sheldon drove his electric cart back through the chicken house, grateful for this means of transportation. Howard Flory had done a super job at customizing the cart for him. Now someone just had to do the same with their car.

After supper, Sheldon discussed his idea with Mary Ellen. He wanted to see what she said about his notion.

"Oh, Sheldon. Do you think you should try this? We don't need you to be hurt worse." Her brow was creased. "I have enough to worry about."

But after some discussion, they decided that Sheldon would call Ira and see what he thought. It wouldn't hurt to try.

"Promise me you'll be careful," Mary Ellen was trying not to allow her fear to hold back her independent husband. She brushed a wisp of hair out of her face. "We need you."

Sheldon picked up the phone and dialed Ira's phone number. He would see what Ira thought. A creative mechanic like Ira would have some idea for how Sheldon could drive his car despite his limitations.

Sheldon laid out his idea and after talking it over for a few minutes, Ira agreed to try. Someone would take the car over to Ira's mechanic shop on Yosemite Avenue next week.

When he got off the phone with Ira about customizing his car, Sheldon called his uncle Jay to see if someone could take the station wagon over to Ira's shop.

"Yes," replied Jay heartily. "We will take care of it. I'll let you know for sure when."

The station wagon was taken to Ira Denlinger's place where he planned to tinker with it and ultimately design a way for Sheldon to drive it. Ira was the sole owner and operator of the mechanic shop. He was a very particular man and known for his excellent work.

After almost a week of waiting, Ira called and asked Sheldon to come and test his idea. Sheldon watched impatiently out the window for Merven to come pick him up. He tried to shift his heavy body in the wheelchair by bracing his arms on the armrests to lift himself a few inches. *I guess this is the closest I can get to pacing,* he thought in sardonic amusement. This would potentially be his first time driving in almost two years. Would he be coordinated enough? Strong enough?

Sheldon slid into Merven's blue Buick from his wheelchair. Merven folded the chair, placed it in the back seat, and closed the door. He scooted into his seat beside Sheldon and started the car. A honey bee buzzed in the window and Sheldon swatted at it with his stronger right hand.

It was a twenty-minute drive south through Modesto to the mechanic shop, but since there was little traffic they made it in good time. Merven pulled off the street and drove around the hedge and to the shop behind Ira's house. Ivy grew up across the building and across the eaves and hung down like green icicles. Several yellow chrysanthemums were blooming at one corner.

Sheldon took the smooth wooden board from the car seat and turned toward the wheelchair which Merven had positioned beside the car. He slid into his wheelchair and wheeled himself over to his own car, peering into the window. A grey tomcat appeared from nowhere to rub against Sheldon's leg. The cat arched his back, whined a meow, and looked toward the shop. The sound of a tool clattered from within the shop.

If Ira wasn't working on cars, he was cleaning his shop. He always had an organized garage and work shelves. "That way I can find my tools," he said. "If I want to search for something, it should not be for a tool or part, it should be for treasures or Scriptures."

"There he is," said Merven, glancing toward the shop.

Ira strode out from the shop's open garage door, wiping his hands on a clean rag. He involuntarily ducked as he passed through the doorway. His white hair shone in the California sunshine. The grey cat disappeared under the car.

"Hello, Brother Sheldon," he called.

Sheldon raised his hand in greeting and smiled, "Are you ready for the Second Coming, brother?"

"Watching and praying," Ira replied as he opened the car door. "I oiled the door hinge so it wouldn't squeak." He smiled. "I hope it works for you. Take a peek and see what you think."

Ira explained how he had welded an extension rod and had installed another accelerator so that Sheldon could operate the accelerator with his stronger left foot. Ira had devised a hand brake that Sheldon could push with his left thumb. He would steer with his stronger right arm only.

"I am anxious to try it out." Sheldon's excitement showed in his voice. Placing his wooden board between his wheelchair and the car seat, he grabbed the handle Ira had fixed on the side and slid himself toward his seat. He then grabbed the steering wheel to continue sliding into place behind the wheel. Sheldon blinked back tears as he grasped the steering wheel. *Maybe I really will be able to drive again.*

Merven folded the wheelchair and placed it behind the driver's seat. Sheldon laid his smooth board next to himself on the seat. He pumped the accelerator and turned the key. The car coughed and sputtered to life.

"Oh, I forgot to ask what I owe," Sheldon murmured to himself. He quickly turned the car off. He leaned out the window. "What do I owe you, brother? I forgot to ask."

"Nothing." Ira waved his hand. "I enjoyed the challenge. I just hope it works for you." His steel blue eyes twinkled as he smiled. "If any of it needs to be adjusted or remade, let me know and I'll redo it for you."

Sheldon drove out the narrow gravel lane to the street as the other two men watched. He turned onto Yosemite Avenue and drove his car slowly along the back streets, testing the brakes with his left thumb. It was sensitive and would stop on a dime. He would have to be careful with braking. He would also have to be careful with his balance since he could only use his right hand on the steering wheel. Overall it was working well. A grin spread its way across Sheldon's face, a face that had deep lines drawn by suffering and pain.

As he turned onto Rumble Road, he whistled a tune that was caught away in the wind. He pressed the customized accelerator with his left foot. It was great having a vehicle to drive again. He would no longer have to depend on others as much for transportation now. He felt a tinge of guilt as he thought of how many hours and miles and dollars had been spent to help him. How could he ever repay for all those deeds of kindness? He would figure out some way.

Perhaps a life of determination and gratefulness could somehow inspire someone else in difficulty. He hoped so.

chapter fifteen
A PURPOSE TO LIVE

1961

"Mark," Sheldon called quietly, "Grandpa is here." There was loud knocking on the back door. On Saturdays when Mark was home from school, he would help clean the chicken houses. Coronado, a hired man, used to help, but now Mark was old enough to take his place. They didn't have any extra money for hired labor if it wasn't absolutely necessary.

Grandpa Walter Grover came over and they took out that week's manure. "It is better to keep up with the work than to get behind," Grandpa said in his blunt way. "A stitch in time saves nine!"

At five o'clock Saturday morning Grandpa would pound on the door if Mark wasn't up yet. "Time to get up," he bellowed. "Let's go get at it." Sometimes Sheldon, who was having his quiet time in the living room, had to wheel over to the sixteen-year-old's room and knock on the door.

Soon grandfather and grandson were on their way to the chicken houses. Cool valley air that had not yet been seared by the California sunshine filtered in through the windows and doorways that were now open. A kangaroo rat skidded around the corner as it headed for its hole.

The older man and young boy worked side by side in the warm, dusty building. Not much was said as they worked but each understood what needed to be done.

"Sure is nice having someone who can work," said Walter with a grunt. The shovel scraped along the rough concrete. It caught on a crack and stopped abruptly. He jerked it back and tried again. "Coronado could never keep at it. Always talking about the latest tragedy he read in the *Modesto News*."

Walter and Mark shoveled the manure into wheelbarrows and ran them out to the twenty-foot wooden farm trailer which was backed down into a dugout spot between two of the chicken houses. They pushed their muck-encrusted wheelbarrows up a thick wooden plank to the trailer and dumped the load. Then they returned for more. This boring cycle they continued until the last shovelful had been loaded for the week.

After Sheldon had prepared for the day, he too would be out helping with chores. He wheeled out to the shop where his electric cart was sitting and fully charged, slid into the cart, and headed off to help work.

Walter had already shoved the custom-made feed tub onto his cart. Sheldon bumped along out to the chicken houses. He stopped by the large feed bin and yanked the handle to allow the feed to pour into the box-like tub. Cracked feed mash landed on the growing mound and slid down to the edges until the tub was full.

Sheldon's neck hurt as he strained to feed the chickens and gather the eggs. Almost all the work had to be done with his right arm. His left arm was mostly skin and bones with a little strength in the fingers. A silent groan of effort slipped out of his mouth as he strained to dump another scoop of feed into the feeding troughs attached to the cages.

A fly warmed by the morning sunshine zoomed around Sheldon and landed on his arm. Its little feet tickled his skin. He shook it off but it landed again.

Sheldon was a little jealous as he watched his father and his son work with such ease and skill. Pop always was a hard worker and had experienced the hardships of living in the unpredictable Midwest as well as surviving the Depression days. Mark was a developing young lad with a bright future. Much brighter than his own, he thought in discouragement. What did he have to look forward to besides wheelchairs, improvised methods, and glances of pity?

Surely there's something to be thankful for, thought Sheldon dismally. *Help me, Lord!* He groped desperately for a glimmer of light in his agony. *Yes,* he all but sobbed as he clutched at a thought, *I am thankful for all the help in the many areas of my changed world.* His breath came easier and his mind steadied. *Thank you, my Lord and Savior.* He was also glad for the work ethic of his people that kept them occupied and stable and ready to lend a hand. Another thing he could be thankful for was his close-knit family. Yes, there were things to be thankful for.

Calmed, ready to take up the burden that his life was now, Sheldon quietly moved on with the next task before him. Outwardly there had been no sign of the turmoil that wracked him so unmercifully at unexpected times. *No one needs to know,* he thought firmly.

Soon the chicken manure was loaded onto the wagon and the chicken houses had been cleaned for the week. Walter hooked his pickup to the farm wagon, and he and Mark were off to the home place on Shoemake. As they drove along, the trailer tires hummed fiercely and some of the dry manure flew into the air and settled along the streets. A young lady in a late model Volkswagen blew her horn angrily at the flying excreta.

At the farm Walter parked the pickup and wagon near the big red barn, and brought Sheldon's John Deere crawler and manure spreader and parked it next to the wagon. Now the wagon load of chicken manure could be shoveled onto the spreader.

"Do you think you ever shovel the same shovelful twice?" Grandpa grinned at Mark. He straightened and rubbed his back.

Soon the spreader was full and ready to be taken out to the vineyard or fields. Sometimes Grandpa allowed Mark to drive the tractor between the grapevines to spread the manure. This was always the highlight of the day for Mark.

Sheldon prayed often for his sons and daughters. He thought of the verses in the Psalms: "Thy wife shall be as a fruitful vine by the sides of thine house: thy children like olive plants round about thy table. Behold, that thus shall the man be blessed that feareth the Lord. The Lord shall bless thee out of Zion."[1]

Sometimes the hours dragged by for Sheldon, but with his continuous prayer to the Lord he could manage to keep working. He dreamed up new ways to manage difficulty and obstacles. After all, he needed to keep bread on the table for his wife and youngsters and meet the expenses of a growing family.

How can I help my children feel worthwhile, without requiring a lot of money? Sheldon thought. He knew how it felt to be a teenager at the lower end of the peer group. He wanted somehow to teach the importance of contentment and at the same time help them experience the satisfaction of success.

All the children would be going to school that fall. Harold, who would be six years old and in first grade, would be attending Stanislaus Union Elementary School with Becky. Mark and Marilyn would be studying at Modesto High School.

Sheldon was pleased that his children could get a higher education than he had gotten. He wanted to help his children in every way he could to grow up as productive Californians. Even if all his dreams were not realized in himself, they could be realized in his children. So when Mark approached him about a place to raise hogs, Sheldon had a suggestion.

"Why don't you build pens between and behind the chicken houses," he responded. "You can raise your pigs there and then you can supply us with meat each year for your rent."

Mark was overjoyed. He went to work immediately to build pens and find some breeding stock. Sheldon helped where he could.

One cool evening in February, Mary Ellen pulled the bedroom door shut as they prepared for bed. She closed the curtains and pulled back the comforter and sheets.

---

[1] Psalm 128: 3-5

"Sheldon."

Sheldon looked up quickly as Mary Ellen spoke. Her voice was lined with fear and anxiety. She looked older than her almost thirty-six years of age. She sat on the edge of the bed.

"Yes, dear," he said.

"I think we are going to have another baby. I believe it will be due around our anniversary."

"On our anniversary? That would be great."

Sheldon stopped rolling in his wheelchair. A draft from the slightly open window caused the light blue curtain to move against the little desk. The only sound besides Mary Ellen's breathing was the ticking clock.

"This is dangerous, Sheldon. You need me. The children need me. You know how risky this will be." She dropped her head and hot tears fell into her lap. Sheldon wheeled closer to the bed and took Mary Ellen's hands into his. He sat quietly breathing a silent prayer.

"Let's pray, dear." Sheldon's quiet voice was sober now. "I didn't mean to be lighthearted about it."

As they prayed and brought their fear and distress to their heavenly Father, a Presence filled the room. Gone was the uncertainty of the future and in its place was a great calm. God had visited them. He would be with them.

"Thank you for praying, Sheldon," Mary Ellen pulled out her crumpled hanky and blew her nose and wiped her eyes. Her shoulders lifted and fell with a deep sigh.

"I love you, Mary Ellen, and God will see us through." That night the two slept deeply under the shadow of the Almighty.

The summer passed with Mary Ellen needing more rest because of the heat and her progressing pregnancy. Marilyn and Becky were able to help much more with the household work and cooking. Mark was working hard to feed and fatten his pigs. And Harold continued to entertain everyone with his boyish talents and mischievousness. There was always something for everyone to do.

"Becky," called Mary Ellen, "could you take your bicycle and go down to

Woodbridge Market and get two pounds of hamburger for us?"

To get to the market, the children rode down Rumble Road to Dale Road. Then they cut across Grandpa Rumble's property to the market facing Route 99. It may have been a mile taking this route to the market, but at least most people along these streets were friends and church folks.

As it was nearing the date for the baby's birth, Marilyn and Becky helped more with the housework to relieve Mama. Sheldon was glad for hardworking children who pitched in and made up for his and Mary Ellen's inabilities.

"Mama, what's wrong?" asked Marilyn in concern. She had just arrived home from school. Harold and Becky were already out in the egg room and Mama was alone.

Mary Ellen wiped her eyes and turned her head. Marilyn moved a little closer.

"Daddy wanted the baby on our anniversary. Today."

"Oh, Mama. That's okay. He didn't mean anything bad by that. It would have been neat, but I'm sure it's not that important to him."

"I wanted to please him—to give him his wish." Mary Ellen sadly picked up the spatula to continue spreading the icing on the cake she was making. She continued to struggle with depression occasionally.

"Daddy will love you regardless, Mama."

"I'm sorry, Marilyn. I shouldn't have been crying over something so small."

Marilyn gave her mother a big hug. "We love you, Mama."

On September 28, the day after Sheldon and Mary Ellen's anniversary, their fifth child and third son was born. They called him Robert. *Another olive plant around the table*, thought Sheldon with deep satisfaction. *The Lord is good to all that fear him.*

They were glad for another healthy child. It had been a beautiful birth, another answer to prayer. They had dreamed of a family and now it was reality. They hadn't dreamed of wheelchairs and improvised methods of living, but this was their life and God was with them. He had always been with them whether times were good or not so good.

But the strain of childbirth and extra work loads because of a handicapped husband resulted in another long and severe bout of post-partum depression for Mary Ellen. Sometimes she stayed in bed with her face to the wall. Those days were difficult and sobering for the family. But valleys give way to foothills and clouds to sunshine, and so Mary Ellen too found herself up and helping in the home once more after many months.

Soon Robert, who was no longer a baby by this time, was crawling about and had to be watched constantly. He began to pull himself up and try to walk. Sheldon loved watching his son develop. He would call the little one to stand next to his wheelchair and hold on to it. And as he watched, he prayed. He prayed that each one of his children would grow up to follow the Lord and become more than just productive Californians but also citizens of the household and kingdom of God.

Sheldon's growing youngsters gave him a purpose to live. He was thinking about the future of his little ones and how he could meet their needs. He couldn't do as much as other healthy fathers, but he could spend time in prayer for them and God would take care of the rest. As the family grew bigger, the expenses also grew. It was time for more income to keep the bills paid and food on the table. He would need to do some checking around for something more to do. Perhaps a factory job. His spirit groaned at the thought; he had always been an outdoors person. But circumstances had changed. Adapting was the word he must live by now, like it or not. He set his jaw more firmly.

chapter sixteen
B&B TRUCKING

1965

The blazing ball of fire disappeared over the horizon and darkness crept slowly over Modesto, California. Inside the Grover home, the evening meal was over, the table scrubbed, and the family was beginning to settle in for the night. Mark and Marilyn were sitting in the living room reading quietly, and Becky was occupied with embroidery work. Harold and Robert had been tucked into bed, and Sheldon and Mary Ellen were now in their bedroom huddled around the little desk.

"So, how are we going to pay the electric bill, dear? The income from the hens is just not enough anymore." Sheldon clenched his teeth. "I have to find another job. Maybe a night job."

"Sheldon! You can't do that."

"Why? At least I can try."

Sheldon looked at his wife with such steely determination that she laughed.

"I imagine that one of these days you will try to climb Half Dome again to prove you can do it." She laid her hand on his arm. "I wish I could do more."

"Let's sleep on it, dear. And pray, of course."

Sheldon could hear Mary Ellen's light breathing as she slept. He tried to roll into a more bearable position. Later, he heard the clock chime one o'clock. Finally, he fell asleep, but had a dream that the electric company came and shut off the power to their home, that the air conditioner stopped running and Mary Ellen began to faint.

"No. *No!*" The strangled moan came from his lips.

"Sheldon! Wake up. Are you having a nightmare, or what's happening?" Mary Ellen nudged him gently.

"Huh? What?" He groaned. He had thought Mary Ellen was fainting because of the heat. It must have been a dream.

"It was just a dreadful dream." His voice was raspy with sleep.

Sheldon fell asleep again, but this time did not remember anything until his alarm went off. He twisted, stretched to the side, and picked up the ringing alarm. It was four o'clock. He shut it off and worked his way to the edge of the bed. *I can do all things through Christ which strengtheneth me,* he thought. *I must get up. Perhaps the Lord will return today!* The thought gave him energy.

After he had spent an hour dressing and preparing for the day, he wheeled to the living room to read some Scripture. As he prayed, the thought of bookkeeping kept hovering in the back of his mind. *Maybe God is showing me an opportunity to work with accounting,* he thought. *This would be something I could do at home in the evenings, or even during the day when I'm not out in the poultry houses.* Excitement began to build as his inventive mind weighed options. *I have always taken detailed records of my own finances, so why couldn't I be an accountant or bookkeeper for someone else?*

Sheldon wheeled outside to check his garden. It was cool and refreshing this early in the morning. He slid into his cart, which was charged fully by then. Birds were twittering thither and yon. Somewhere in the distance, a heavy truck rumbled along, probably hauling a load of watermelons to the packing sheds.

After turning on the sprinklers to their garden, he drove out to see whether the hens needed water. Sheldon worked for an hour before Becky came to tell him that breakfast was on the table. As he drove back to the house, the electric cart bounced over a stray stone and jerked the steering wheel. Sheldon grabbed it to balance himself. These sudden jerks always sent twinges of pain stabbing through his body. It happened often throughout the day, and he was becoming accustomed to the pain. That didn't make it less painful, but it was easier to manage life when he expected to hurt. This was simply his reality now.

The scrambled eggs and fried potatoes were steaming as Sheldon rolled up to the table. Eggs were plentiful, as the family ate all those that were cracked or imperfect and could not be sold. As often as not, the breakfast menu included eggs.

Marilyn laid down a few paper napkins and four-year-old Robert beat his spoon on the table. Becky brought a pitcher of iced tea and set it on the table.

"Sorry, the tea isn't sweet this morning," said Becky. "We're out of sugar again."

"How are you doing, Daddy?" asked Mark as he sat down. "Anything I can do before I leave?" At nineteen years, Mark was now taller than his mother, with a shock of dark brown hair swept neatly into place. His blue eyes revealed his concern, although there was also a glint of youthfulness present that wasn't exactly begging for anything too difficult to do.

"Actually, I've been thinking that my electric cart needs a wash sometime," Sheldon replied. His blue eyes twinkled. He locked the brakes on his wheelchair. "Maybe you could wash it before you go."

"I think I have time to do that before I leave," said Mark. He cleared his throat. "Should I use soap?"

"Yes, and a stiff brush."

"Breakfast is ready," Mary Ellen took her seat next to Sheldon. They bowed their heads as Sheldon gave a blessing.

"I have an idea concerning what we discussed last evening," he remarked as he reached for a piece of toast.

"Tell me about it," Mary Ellen invited as she dished some eggs onto his plate.

"I've been thinking about accounting. I could get some training somewhere and work out of our home. Maybe put a sign out by the road?"

"Where will you get training?" Mary Ellen's eyes lifted inquiringly. "And when will you do it?"

"Maybe I can go to an evening class. I can do some research. Maybe a correspondence course."

"Can I go along too?" Harold asked as he took a big gulp of tea. The wiry ten-year-old set his glass down too quickly, and a bit of tea splashed onto the table.

After praying more about the idea, making a few phone calls, and talking with some of the church brothers, they decided that Sheldon would go to evening classes to learn about accounting and bookkeeping.

Sheldon enrolled in the Modesto Junior College, which held evening classes. He looked forward to his studies. He had stopped school after the eighth grade, which had been a disappointment to him, though he had enjoyed working with his father. Going to college for the evening classes would be different, but he was sure he would enjoy it.

Mary Ellen or Marilyn took Sheldon to the college downtown, only a ten- or fifteen-minute drive. The classes were between 6 and 9 p.m. When they arrived at the college, someone would help him get into his wheelchair, and then open the doors to the building so he could get inside to find his classes.

As Marilyn had other motives, she often took Sheldon to his classes; after she dropped him off, she would go to the post office downtown to mail a letter to her boyfriend, Rodney Gish, who lived out of town.

After the course was over, and he had obtained his certificate, Sheldon began accounting and bookkeeping. His business never seemed to take off very well, however, and he largely did bookkeeping.

One Sunday morning as he was leaving church, Don Beachler stopped him. His six-foot frame overshadowed Sheldon. He stuck out a friendly hand.

"Brother Sheldon. Blessings."

"To you as well." Sheldon shook his hand.

"Sheldon, I need a bookkeeper."

"Don, I need a job."

After a short conversation, they planned to meet at Don's office the next day to discuss the job description and what Don would expect from him. The Modesto ash trees rustled in the wind and a group of women on the church steps laughed and talked. Families piled into their cars to head home.

Sheldon talked about the new job opportunity with Mary Ellen as they drove out of the church parking lot. Robert and Harold pulled each other's hair and tussled in the back seat as the adults discussed the future.

"I think this is a godsend, don't you, dear?"

"It seems to be. We have been praying." She smiled at him. "Maybe this is God's answer?" Sheldon's thumb hit the brakes as a grey fox dashed across the road and disappeared into the hedge along the street.

The next morning, Sheldon drove out to Don Beachler's business on Standiford Road. The company was called B&B Trucking, and Don had started it to do custom grain harvesting and trucking.

After seeing the offices and discussing his job description, Sheldon agreed to take the position. He was grateful for a good job with a brother from his church. God had answered his prayer in supplying this job to help support his family. Now with the income from the laying hens and his day job, they should be able to keep current with their bills. Maybe they could actually close the egg business soon, as the children were finding partners and leaving the nest.

Sheldon worked every day except Sundays and days that he had an appointment with his doctor or therapist. Sometimes he would work right through his lunch break because of the amount of bookkeeping that needed to be done. To keep him going, he munched on a bag of carrots or some fresh fruit. At least if he had something to chew on, he wouldn't need to grind his teeth as often because of the pain that gnawed at his body.

He and Don often talked about the Scriptures and shared their struggles. Sometimes, Sheldon gently rebuked Don for being too harsh with a driver or employee. Over the years, they enjoyed each other's company and developed a deep camaraderie.

Normally, Sheldon was the first man at work, and would wait for Don or an employee to come and push a wheelchair to his car from the office where it was stored. Then he would put down his smooth board and slide from his car to the chair.

After enduring more than a decade of learning how to cope with his handicap, he had also learned either to wait for others or figure out a way to accomplish a task by himself. He disciplined himself to spend the waiting time in meditation and prayer. Quite a change from the hard-driving, self-sufficient man he was formerly. This change came over slow, grinding years of suffering and restraint.

One morning, Sheldon arrived at the office only to wait and wait. *Should I crawl to the office?* he thought. *I could be sitting here all day.*

Finally, a pickup roared into the parking lot and a cloud of dust billowed over Sheldon's car. Harry Rodrian had arrived.

"Good morning, Sheldon. Need a hand?" The friendly face grinned into the window at him.

"No one around this morning, it seems." Sheldon coughed. He could have totaled the receipts in the fine dust that had settled onto his car.

"Yeah, I don't know what's going on. Don and the drivers probably had schedules that either took them out very early or they had something else going."

"I've been here an hour now. Would you be so kind as to retrieve my chair from the office behind the door?" Sheldon sighed. His face was sober. He was still so dependent on others.

Harry soon returned with the wheelchair and positioned it beside the open car door. Sheldon turned to get his board; it wasn't beside him. He looked on the floorboard. No board.

"Sorry, I must have forgotten my sliding board." Sheldon looked down and then at the chair two feet away. "You may need to help me reach my chair, Harry." How he hated to ask for help!

Harry moved next to the car to support Sheldon, and reached under his legs to help him to his chair. A shiver ran through Harry's body. His gut hurt as he helped Sheldon sit in his chair. He had felt only skin and bones for legs.

"Thank you, Harry," Sheldon said quietly. "Would you mind pushing me up to the office door?" Sunlight reflected off the dew-moistened bark of a palm tree nearby. A tree frog flattened against the trunk blended in with the bark as it watched the two men move toward the building.

"Do you have a long day ahead of you?" Sheldon asked as the normally jolly man turned soberly to leave.

"Naw, not a real big day. I need to work on a trailer some crazy driver broke by doing something dumb." He rolled his eyes. "I could wring his neck."

"Hum. I don't think you want to do that," Sheldon said quietly. "It may have been just an accident and not even his fault. I have made plenty of blunders too and wouldn't want anyone to wring my neck every time I did something dumb."

"Well, you may be right, but he needs to be taught a lesson."

"He may have learned his lesson by what happened," Sheldon encouraged with a sigh.

Sheldon often helped drivers work through issues like these, and even gave them advice when they asked. The employees learned to trust Sheldon and his quiet, rock-solid ways, and would confide in him knowing that no one else would ever hear about it. He could keep a secret and would pray for them as well.

Relationships, even in the workplace, were very important to him because he knew that now, more than ever before, he was dependent on other people. There were some things he just couldn't do alone.

Not only did he need help with tasks beyond his reach, but he also loved people just for being who they were. He loved God deeply, and God loved all His children. Loving others only strengthened his relationship with God further. Thus, there were multiple reasons to develop friendships and to respect his fellow men.

Sheldon would soon discover how much he missed a relationship when it was gone.

chapter seventeen
ONE MORE ANSWERED PRAYER

1969

It was a cloudy afternoon with an imperceptible breeze, and even though the sun was blocked from view, it was warm. The palm trees hung their heads without a whisper. The dogwoods, crepe myrtles, and cactus plants were beginning to bloom. It was April in Modesto.

Robert scurried down the almond tree and trotted to the house. He had heard Mama call his name. *I wonder what she wants*, Robert thought. She usually let him play outside longer than this. He hadn't been home from school very long.

He paused on the doorstep for a moment before entering the house as a car pulled into the lane. Daddy was arriving home from work. Likely Robert would need to bring out the wheelchair and push it up to the car, but Mama wouldn't have known he was coming. He ran in through the kitchen to the living room. Mama was lying on the couch.

"Robert, I don't feel well," Mama groaned weakly. "Is Daddy home yet? I thought I just heard someone drive into the lane."

"Yes, Mama. He just came. I should take the wheelchair out."

"That's fine." She turned to find a more comfortable position from the pain. The pain had been increasing ever since she had caught the flu back in January. For some reason, she just couldn't seem to get over the illness, so she had gone to see Doctor Battle. His diagnosis was that she was just weak from her congenital heart disease and had a poor immune system.

Rest, drink lots of liquids, and eat good food was the recommendation. This seemed to always be the recommendation, but now—now she felt worse. Surely she should be feeling better. She did feel slightly better to know that Sheldon was home.

As Sheldon pulled up and parked his car, he saw eight-year-old Robert pause a moment before entering the house. Some days, time seemed to creep for Sheldon, but at other times the days flew by with uncontrollable swiftness. His children were maturing and one by one leaving to begin their own homes. He wouldn't want it any other way, but it was emotionally stretching for him to see his children leaving. At least he still had Harold and Robert around. God certainly had blessed them when He gave them the two youngest children to keep the house lively. Eventually though, he knew that he must let them go, too.

Mark was married to a beautiful and talented young girl named Lorraine Miller. Marilyn's heart had been stolen by Rodney Gish, and now Becky had a boyfriend. It seemed just yesterday that Sheldon had stood with Mary Ellen next to the little cabin on the home place anticipating their life together. He could still see her standing among the wildflowers and weeds around the cabin, the wind playing with a wisp of her hair, and her deep blue eyes longing to spend life with him.

Sheldon didn't have long to wait until Robert came pushing the spotlessly clean silver wheelchair up to the car. He opened his door while Robert held the wheelchair in place and thrust the brakes into position. Robert had done this many times, so it was nothing unusual for him. He knew nothing else. Daddy always had been in a wheelchair as far as he was concerned.

He had actually learned to walk by pulling himself up and hanging on the silver bars of Daddy's chair.

"How's my Robert doing?" asked Sheldon as he grabbed for his smooth board and laid it from the car to the wheelchair.

"Okay, Daddy," Robert's eager young voice piped. "I saw another scrub jay building a nest in the neighbor's almond tree."

"Did you knock it out?" asked Sheldon as he backed away from his car. "They can ruin trees."

"Yes, I did," replied Robert proudly.

Sheldon wheeled up the ramp with Robert pushing from behind. He stopped while Robert opened the door for him so he could enter the boot room. It had been another long day and he was tired. He wondered what was for supper. He didn't smell anything cooking. The window to the kitchen was open a crack, but he hadn't heard any pots or pans clinking as he was coming in.

"Mama's not feeling well, Daddy," said Robert as they entered the house. "She's lying on the couch."

Sheldon took a deep breath and wheeled into the living room to see what he would find. His wife was moaning and her face was ashen.

"Mary Ellen."

"I don't feel well." Mary Ellen groaned. "I don't know if it was something I ate or what. I had called Robert to come help me and then he said you were coming. Sorry I don't have something ready for you to eat but I am just feeling awful."

Sheldon wheeled close to Mary Ellen and took her hand into his. "Don't worry about supper, dear. Becky should be back any time, and Robert and I can maybe start something."

"I am more concerned about you than supper," he continued. "I will need to set up an appointment for you at Dr Battle's to see if he can let us know what is wrong. This has been happening more and more frequently, hasn't it?" The concerned husband chewed his lip, thinking over the past month or so.

"Let's pray and ask for God's help and wisdom," Sheldon said decisively.

He bowed his head. Robert knelt beside his mother. After they had prayed and committed the growing problem to God, a spirit of calmness settled over them. God had answered their prayer and had once more poured out His infinite grace upon them.

"Should I get you an aspirin and a glass of water?" Sheldon asked. Mary Ellen's face was relaxed yet not free from pain.

"That would be good." Mary Ellen responded as she shifted to a better position. The back door banged shut as someone entered.

"Becky's home," Robert called.

Sheldon relaxed just knowing that Becky would be able to make a meal. He could help but didn't know the slightest thing about cooking. He had never needed to learn since either his mother or sisters or wife always surrounded him. And now since he was handicapped, it made learning even more difficult. Hopefully he never would need to know how, he thought.

That night Mary Ellen dozed fitfully and was restless; however, in the morning she felt slightly better. Sheldon arranged with Don Beachler to take off from work, and then called the doctor's office to make an appointment.

At the hospital, the staff conducted more tests and did further investigating, but they could find nothing that was seriously wrong. Continue resting and drinking lots of liquids, the couple was told. A prescription painkiller was given to reduce the pain if needed.

Sheldon and Mary Ellen left the hospital and stopped by the pharmacy to pick up the prescription. The tall, blond pharmacist took the paper with nearly illegible writing and turned to get a package.

Even though Sheldon outwardly appeared calm, he felt angry. Surely there was a better way to find out what the problem was. If they continued to do the same things, they would simply get the same results. *We don't need painkillers. We need to get to the bottom of the problem. The root problem,* he thought in irritation.

The pain and illness persisted during the spring months and into the summer. The boys were out of school now and could help around the house, and Becky helped out too when she wasn't with her boyfriend.

Mark and Lorraine passed through their own valley when they discovered they would not be able to have children. Sheldon and Mary Ellen grieved with them in their hour of disappointment but were overjoyed to hear that they had found a little boy to adopt. Tiny two-month-old Peter joined Rodney and Marilyn's cute little daughter Marybeth as the second grandchild.

"Dear Father," Sheldon prayed during the day as he worked in the office at B&B Trucking, "please give us wisdom to know how to proceed." The joy of children and grandchildren helped alleviate the sorrow they often experienced, but it did not outweigh the grief of watching his wife suffer.

A few verses came back to Sheldon as he worked. He had been trying to memorize them and kept his Bible open to the passage. He read and recited them again. "For which cause we faint not; but though our outward man perish, yet the inward man is renewed day by day. For our light affliction, which is but for a moment, worketh for us a far more exceeding and eternal weight of glory; while we look not at the things which are seen, but at the things which are not seen: for the things which are seen are temporal; but the things which are not seen are eternal."[1]

It brought Sheldon some comfort to know that this would be "but for a moment." *Pain still hurts, though*, he mused. His own experience told him that.

It hurt him deeply to see Mary Ellen's condition and her lack of progress in recovering. He needed her now more than ever. He wasn't getting any younger and he couldn't lose her. He had contracted polio. It had wrecked his body. Wasn't that enough trouble for him? Didn't God know when to stop? He wiped his brow, which was beaded with an agonizing sweat. His mind grappled for some assurance. He thought again of the verse, "And we know that all things work together for good to them that love God, to them who are the called according to his purpose."[2] He exhaled deeply and shook himself. He would have to trust that God had a purpose in all of this.

---

[1] 2 Corinthians 4:16-18
[2] Romans 8:28

Weeks turned into months and Mary Ellen did not improve. Finally, Sheldon, Mark, and Mary Ellen's father Joseph requested that the doctors do more extensive testing and scans to discover what was causing the increasing weakness.

It was a mild summer evening in mid-June when Mary Ellen was taken to the Memorial Hospital in Ceres. After checking in around 8 p.m., she was shown to her own room. A simple hospital cot was pushed up against one wall. A light was suspended on a retractable arm above her, and a shiny black telephone was stuck on the wall above the headboard. After Sheldon and the other family members left, Mary Ellen tried to relax and study the Scriptures. She dozed off but couldn't sleep deeply. She awoke early in the morning.

At mid-forenoon, a nurse came to take Mary Ellen for more x-rays and testing. Mary Ellen laid her new Bible on the stand beside her bed. She had been marking her favorite verses in the Bible and reading a few passages. She was thankful for the Word of God to sustain her at such a difficult time as this.

"Can you get up or should I help you?" asked Rene, the attending nurse. Her smooth face gleamed as if she had rubbed baby oil on it, and her eyebrows were pencil perfect. The white uniform she wore appeared as if it were stiff enough to stand by itself, and her short nursing cap perched upon her head at an audacious angle.

"Can you steady me so I can reach the chair?" requested Mary Ellen as she stretched out her hand. "I think I can walk okay. I am just very thirsty and hungry."

"Yes. Sorry you can't eat or drink. It's the rule when you go for this type of x-ray."

The nurse wheeled Mary Ellen down the corridors to the x-ray room. After having almost one hundred photos taken and lying for two hours on the table bed, she was released. Mary Ellen felt much better when she had returned to her room and bathed. She dressed and lay down to relax.

A knock sounded on her door.

"Come in," Mary Ellen called. The door was pushed open, and Becky appeared with her boyfriend Harold Long close behind.

"Mama, how is it going?" Becky gave her mother a hug and kiss.

"I just bathed and dressed, so I feel better," replied Mary Ellen with a sigh. "The nurses and doctors are nice enough. This morning, though, I was not allowed to eat since they had planned to do special x-rays on me. Hopefully I will get some food soon."

"Shall I go ask?" Becky's eyes filled with concern.

"Surely they know you are back now," said Harold. "They should be coming soon."

Sure enough, when Becky reached the door and opened it, a nurse stood outside with a tray.

"Excuse me," she said. "I have a light meal for the patient. May I enter?"

While Mary Ellen ate the simple meal and rested, Becky and Harold took turns reading poems and Scripture for her. *It is so beautiful and refreshing to have loved ones come to encourage me,* Mary Ellen thought. She wished it were easier for Sheldon to be with her, though.

During the afternoon, Grandpa and Grandma Rumble stopped in to say hello. Fanny Beachler and Alice Woodbridge also stopped by to chat a bit.

Not long after Harold and Becky left, a bouquet of flowers was brought to her room. They had been sent from the florist. Mary Ellen read the note included.

> *Dear Mary Ellen,*
>
> *We love you and are praying for you. Don't be discouraged, for the Lord will lift you up.*
>
> *Love,*
> *Grandma and Grandpa Rumble*

Mary Ellen's eyes smarted and a tear slipped over the side of her cheek. So many were thinking about her. They really cared. How different it would be outside the church. Even though pain stabbed through her body, a warm feeling circled her heart and soothed her thoughts.

"Thank you, God," she said aloud.

The next day Doctor Allen came to let Mary Ellen know that they discovered one side of her throat was not functioning properly, and that her vagus nerve was giving her problems. Thirty minutes later, Doctor Metge came in to explain that Mary Ellen's vagus nerve may have been her problem all these years. "When your vagus nerve was overstimulated, it caused your heart to slow down and then you felt weak," he said. The doctor went on to describe in detail what was happening. But weightier news was yet to come.

With more testing and observation, the doctors discovered cancer around Mary Ellen's aorta, a place where surgery could not be done. *Cancer!* Even worse, inoperable cancer. Surely God wouldn't allow such a blow to this family, already staggering under the weight of burdens that seemed too heavy to bear. Sheldon and Mary Ellen sat in stunned silence.

The doctors recommended chemotherapy and multiple treatments of radiation to the area around her heart. After weeks of treatment, Mary Ellen started feeling better though she longed for her home and family. She didn't like staying at the hospital and restlessness began to set in.

And then, after being in the hospital nearly a month, Mary Ellen was suddenly dismissed to go home. *I suppose they have done all they could,* thought Sheldon, submerging his distress as he had learned to do on his own behalf. But thankfully the treatments had helped and Mary Ellen was up and around again.

"I am glad Mama is better," said Robert as he threw his lunch box on the counter. He had just gotten off the bus from school.

"Yes, Robert, I feel some better and I hope it will last." Mary Ellen was sitting in her rocking chair.

Recovering from her hospital stay, Mary Ellen helped around the house as much as could be expected. Sometimes her breathing was heavy and she needed to lie down and rest. Becky was able to make some meals, and Mary Ellen's mother Flossie stopped by frequently.

"How's my buddy?" asked Flossie, tousling Robert's sandy brown hair. She had stopped by to drop off supper that included a casserole ready to go into the oven.

"Hi, Grandma," said Harold, bursting in the door. "Did you bring something to eat? That bus ride is just too long. I am famished."

Sheldon and Mary Ellen loved to see their children growing and active. Sometimes it troubled Mary Ellen to think that she might not be able to see her children much longer. *Maybe God will work a miracle*, she thought hopefully.

Mary Ellen felt better than she had a few months earlier. The terrible pain had been reduced and she could now be up and about. With a mother and wife back in the home, things seemed more normal again for the family. Sheldon, especially, was joyful at the turn of events.

But his hopes were dashed as Mary Ellen began to struggle with breathing again in September. Early one morning as Sheldon was getting dressed for the day, he heard his wife call for him. She had stayed in bed to try and get a little more rest.

"Dear, I can't breathe. You may need to call the doctor." Strained gasps came from Mary Ellen.

Sheldon quickly called the doctor and told him what was happening.

"I'll send an ambulance out right away," he responded.

At the hospital they discovered fluid around Mary Ellen's heart. They drained a quart and a half from her heart cavity. The fluid had crowded her heart over to the right and was also affecting her vagus nerve. They gave her a mustard treatment at the same time, putting some of the mustard into the heart cavity. This treatment was very painful for Mary Ellen, and this time the doctor's diagnoses were quite clear—she didn't have very long to live.

Sheldon again returned home with a leaden heart. During the week, after work or at any other opportunity he could find, he would drive in to see Mary Ellen. Becky was able to make meals and wash clothes. Harold and Robert, ages fourteen and eight, pitched in to help where they could.

"Daddy," asked Robert wistfully. "When will Mama get better?"

"I don't know," Sheldon answered heavily. He feared telling his sons the truth about their mother. She might never get better. She *wouldn't* get better, unless God intervened somehow.

One morning Sheldon awoke and lay thinking about his wife. He prayed desperately for her recovery. He went about the laborious task of getting up and reached for his Bible. He read in Psalm 118, "They compassed me about like bees . . . thou hast thrust sore at me that I might fall: but the LORD helped me." A peace flooded Sheldon's soul, and he felt that God was speaking to him. His heart lightened as he dressed and prepared for the trip out to see Mary Ellen.

As Sheldon drove to the hospital, he sang. Wheeling in to the hospital room, he saw Mary Ellen's sister Lois sitting next to the bed on a swivel recliner reading. She had stayed with her sister overnight. After greeting them, Sheldon opened his Bible. He wheeled closer to the suspended light and read the Psalm 118 verses to them, sharing with his wife and Lois what God had revealed to him. Otherworldly calm filled the room and they all felt God speaking to them.

"I believe that God has answered my prayer," he said. "He is answering *our* prayers."

Sure enough, Mary Ellen immediately began to improve. It wasn't long before the hospital staff began to talk about the miracle in Room 107.

Sheldon was elated as he thought of God's goodness to him in healing his dear wife. His heart sang with praise. He was thankful for a good job, a godly boss, and a steady income. He had so much to be thankful for!

And now something occurred that had become characteristic of this man confined to a wheelchair by paralysis and pain; he began to think about the hurt someone else was feeling. His mind went to his sister Frieda, whose husband had divorced her for another woman. This had been very difficult for Frieda. Perhaps it was worse than having a companion die. Maybe he could do something for his sister. He knew he couldn't do much in his situation, with his polio, but perhaps he could be creative and think of some way to help.

chapter eighteen
AUNT FRIEDA

1970

Another day was dawning on Lambert Avenue as Frieda Denlinger arose. It was dark with a little bit of hazy morning light filtering in through the curtains into her bedroom. She arose with a heavy heart to dress for the day.

Every morning, it seemed, was the same. Get up alone. Eat breakfast alone—that is, if she even ate breakfast.

How long had it been since Delmer had divorced her? Too long. But which was worse, living with someone unfaithful or living in an empty house? When she had her daughters at home with her, it was at least bearable.

But now both of her daughters were married. They had their own lives to live. She was glad that at least they had chosen to be baptized and join the church.

And since Delmer had left, things just weren't the same as they used to be. Her income level was lower now, but she was grateful for the church and its support during these difficult years.

Pop swung by quite often to see if she needed help since he was going past anyway on his trips to and from Sheldon's place up on Rumble Road. Pop did so much for them all even if he seemed a bit rough around the edges at times. He had a good heart underneath that outer brusque nature.

It's too bad Sheldon and Mary Ellen are having such a time of it, she thought to herself. *Sheldon confined to a wheelchair with polio and Mary Ellen in and out of the hospital with cancer and heart problems.* She felt so bad for them. As far as her own health, she was thankful to be doing well except for occasional back problems.

She dressed in her favorite dress. After donning her prayer covering, she went to the living room for some quiet time. She ate breakfast, and then headed for her job at the Downy High School.

After a day at work, Frieda arrived back at her little house on Lambert Street. Today she checked the mail and saw only one envelope. Her heart leapt. It was the third time this kind of envelope came. She hurried to the house, letting the wooden screen door slam, something she never did on any normal day.

Grabbing her scissors, she slit open the envelope. Out fell a check and a letter from the Modesto Church Charity Fund. The church had given money again. Was it from an individual, she wondered, or had the deacons suggested it? It didn't really matter. It was money and would cover the unpaid electric bill that was sitting on her kitchen counter. It would also help with her mortgage, which she had almost paid off.

Even though she had a good job at the cafeteria, her income just didn't cover all the expenses and mortgage. Especially if she had repairs on her little car. Frieda poured herself a cup of orange juice and sat down again to study the letter. Someone cared.

She had been very surprised when Don Miller had offered to build a house for her and finance it too. What a huge relief to know she would have a place to call home after having rented for so many years. Now a couple of checks from someone gave her even more hope for her future.

She had heard her daughters' families were contemplating a move from the German Baptists to a more nominal congregation. Would she stay or go with them? She loved her people and didn't want to leave although, despite their kindness, she felt shame all these years for being a divorcee. She couldn't help it, of course. It hadn't been her choice. Her heart ached just thinking about Delmer's unfaithfulness.

She didn't know if a check from the church fund would come again, but this one had come just in time. Her appreciation for God's people, her people, swelled along with a gentle warm sensation within her breast. God was good and so was the church. He had always provided and He would still.

Maybe it was one of the wealthy businessmen of the church that had done this through the Modesto Fund, Frieda continued to muse. *Oh well, it didn't really matter. It was God providing for her needs.*

/ /

After another day of work, Sheldon wheeled out to his car and opened the door. He slid from his wheelchair into the car. Soon he was on his way home.

It had been a good day and he was glad that he had finished recording the receipts for the month. The more he accomplished, the better it made him feel.

Don always had mounds of work waiting for Sheldon, so he never had to worry about a lack of projects. On the contrary, he usually worried that he wouldn't finish it all. "Job security," David Metzger had called it one day. "It's like housework," David continued with a smirk, "it never gets done."

Sheldon was glad that there was enough income now to pay the bills and start a savings account. He wanted to be able to give more. Somehow giving and serving brought genuine healing to the losses he had experienced.

He had learned that giving was not only enjoyable but also healthy. To only receive and never to give was to become a Dead Sea. All the water it received, it kept; unlike the Sea of Galilee, which gave as much or more than it received.

This was a beautiful picture of what he wanted to become. He was learning to be content with his lot, but wanted to develop into a better person who reflected God's glory.

When Sheldon arrived home, it was unusually cloudy and breezy. *Maybe we will get a bit of rain,* he thought. The orchards and garden needed moisture. If it rained, he wouldn't be able to work in his garden or any other project outdoors. Maybe he could work on his own financial reports and bookkeeping, he thought.

As Sheldon balanced their checkbook, he saw that it was near the date of the month to send a donation again to his sister. The money was sent to the Modesto Church Charity Fund, so the recipient wouldn't know where it was from and the giver could remain anonymous. Sheldon smiled as he wrote out the amount that he and Mary Ellen had agreed upon. He had heard that she wanted to pay off her house mortgage, but with unexpected medical bills and other unforeseen expenses, it seemed nearly impossible.

The money would give Frieda hope when life seemed hopeless. Since her husband had divorced her, he was sure that life was difficult and lonely. What if he were living alone without Mary Ellen? He pushed the thought away from him with a shudder of apprehension.

chapter nineteen
LOVED AND LOST

1970–1971

It was the early spring of 1970 when Mary Ellen hesitantly revealed to Sheldon that she was experiencing a little bit of pain in her side again. Her ribs had begun to bother her and she felt some discomfort.

Not again, Sheldon thought in dismay. He dreaded what this might mean.

As the weeks passed, it soon became too painful for her even to chuckle. It was obvious that she would need to go back to the hospital for a checkup and more testing.

"It appears the cancer has moved to your ribs," Doctor Battle said as he observed a photo. "But we do have a drug called Cytoxin that may help."

"Can I handle this drug?" Mary Ellen asked weakly. She groaned and tried to shift to a more comfortable position.

"Some people can handle it and some can't," he answered. "I guess we will just need to try." He scribbled something on his notepad and left.

Hospitals were becoming almost normal for Mary Ellen. If it wasn't for one reason, it was for another. Mark and Rodney's families often came in to stay overnight or just visit, usually bringing the grandchildren to play in the room with Mary Ellen.

But the Cytoxin worked, and Mary Ellen improved so much that she was able to go home—for a few months. Then Sheldon and Mary Ellen both caught the flu in May. Mary Ellen's ravaged immune system couldn't handle the sickness and kept getting worse and worse. Even in the hospital nothing seemed to help with her declining condition.

Sheldon was working in the office at B&B Trucking when someone called. The hospital staff thought that Mary Ellen wouldn't make it through that night.

"You may want to bring your family in," the doctor said quietly.

So this was it? Had the final, wrenching time come? Was the tie that had blended two lives into one to be rent, torn asunder? Heavily, sorrowfully, Sheldon gathered his keys and wheeled with slumped shoulders to his car. Tears blurred his vision as he cried out to the only Source of help he knew.

That evening, all the family was there, singing for Mary Ellen and reading Scripture for her. As they surrounded her with worship and praise, suddenly Sheldon sensed a calmness come over him.

"It will be okay," the Spirit whispered to his heart. "Go home and get your rest and leave someone here with Mary Ellen because she will get better."

Peace shining from his face, Sheldon motioned for everyone to stop singing and said quietly, "I believe that Mary Ellen will be getting better. Let's have a volunteer stay here with Mary Ellen and watch her while we all go home to get some sleep."

"I'll stay," said Merven, marveling at his brother's quiet confidence. "You all go home and sleep. I had a good day and I feel pretty good. Are you okay with that, Pauline?"

"That will be fine." A touch of wonder lingered in Pauline's smile. "You just stay here with your sister-in-law."

Sheldon was grateful as he drove home with the boys.

"Mama will be fine," he said confidently to Harold and Robert as he motored through Modesto. "God will be with her. Let's sleep well, and I'll go back in the morning to check up on her."

Stars twinkled in the clear night sky and Modesto lay silent except for an occasional passing vehicle. A cleaning lady at the bank was closing her car door, and a murmur could be heard from a few youths infringing on their curfew at the park. A drunk staggered along a downtown street.

Sheldon and the boys slept well and got up to greet a clear and cool morning. Becky helped Harold and Robert pack their lunches for school.

"Have a nice day, boys," Sheldon called after them.

"Becky, will you be at home today?" Sheldon asked as he wheeled through the kitchen to leave. He pulled his jacket on.

"I'll plan to catch up on the house cleaning," answered Becky.

Mary Ellen improved and was able to return home ten days before Becky's wedding. Sheldon was delighted that she was able to be at home. Deep within him, he sensed that she might not be around much longer and that God was lending her for a little while longer. He brushed away these thoughts that were lined with sadness and tried to focus on the present.

There was a flurry of activity at the Grovers' house as they prepared for the special occasion. Everyone pitched in and helped prepare for Becky's wedding.

Windows were washed until they fairly sparkled, and floors were swept multiple times. The entire house experienced an extra dusting and furniture was moved more than once.

The west side of the house was landscaped to brighten the area where the service and ceremony were to be held. Mark, who had started Grover Landscaping earlier that year, helped with the landscaping and design. He lived just down the street from his parents. With his efforts, trees, shrubs, grasses, and flowers soon graced the edges of the lawn and house.

Harold Long and Becky Grover were married on June 20, 1970, in the newly landscaped area on the home place. Mary Ellen, overjoyed that she could be at the wedding, was able to walk down the aisle between the guests for the ceremony. During the service, she sat in a swivel recliner that someone had brought to the wedding as a gift for Harold and Becky. The recliner was soft and allowed her to enjoy the message and the singing.

As Sheldon sat in his wheelchair taking in the wedding service, he was thankful that another one of his children had started a godly home. He prayed that they would be faithful to the heritage endowed them and to God's Word. Who knew what was in store for God's people? He often read up on the news of Israel and contemplated end-time events. Would his children get to see Jesus' Second Coming?

In a few hours it was all over. The marriage ceremony had been performed, the snack served and eaten, and Mr. and Mrs. Harold Long had set out on their wedding trip. After the flurry of activity was over, Sheldon and Mary Ellen sat together and enjoyed the beautiful afternoon. Harold and Robert raced around on their bikes, playing bike tag and calling to their parents.

Since Becky's husband Harold was attending Foothill College and working at Stanford Hospital, both in nearby Santa Clara, the newlyweds decided to start their life in the city. They found a house they could live in while Harold went to college and studied respiratory therapy.

/ /

"Let's go see where Harold and Becky live," said Mary Ellen. Three months had passed since the wedding. "I can make the drive. I'm feeling pretty well."

So it was planned that on Saturday they would drive out and see Harold's place. Sheldon drove, with Mary Ellen resting in the back seat and Harold and Robert sitting in front. Suddenly the car started shaking badly, and the rapid shuddering of the car caused the frail woman excruciating pain.

"Oh, Sheldon. Can we somehow drive slower?" Mary Ellen groaned.

Nonetheless the shaking continued violently. Finally, Sheldon pulled over to the side of the road.

"Let's pray for this car," he suggested firmly. "I think God can fix this problem."

After they had prayed, they pulled out and continued on their way with the car running smoothly. The noise and vibration had stopped.

The trip was a good one and they enjoyed their time with Harold and

Becky in Santa Clara. The return home was again beautiful with the car running smoothly.

"Thank you, God, for another answered prayer," said Sheldon as they arrived home safely.

But the next morning when Sheldon and the boys went to church, the car was again shaking violently.

"I guess I will need to take the car to Ira," remarked Sheldon above the humming vibration. "But we can be thankful God answered our prayer for Mary Ellen and the trip."

Sheldon and Mary Ellen's lives were back to almost normal—for another year. In August of the next summer, Mary Ellen started feeling weak and sick again and, since she was feeling quite low, Sheldon called the ambulance. As he watched his wife being carried on the stretcher to the ambulance, Sheldon intuitively knew, deep within, that she would not be coming home.

The family took turns staying with Mary Ellen in the hospital, and the hospital staff did what they could to make her comfortable and assist her in her last few days. The family tried to prepare themselves for the inevitable parting. It would be a parting that would be tough to bear, especially for those whose hearts were knit so tightly and fondly. But all must pass through that valley, whether prepared or not.

Unless, of course, the Second Coming would happen first, Sheldon thought. He would welcome that, dreaming of being able to dance for joy with his new legs. He smiled to himself as he thought of jumping and dancing with all his might. He would know how the man at the "Beautiful" gate felt, the one Peter had healed at the Temple in Jerusalem. That man hadn't seemed to care what anyone thought about his jumping and shouting after he was healed.

The families attempted to break the news to their children that Grandma would not be around much longer. It was hard for the little ones to understand.

"Peter," said Mark. "Grandma might not get better."

"But I don't want Grandma to die," said Peter plaintively.

As Sheldon worked during the day at the office, his heart was heavy. He knew Mary Ellen's time for going home to be with her Lord was drawing close, and they would soon be parted. He asked that someone call him if she became too ill.

It was so hard for him to sit and watch his wife suffer so much when he could do nothing to help. He would just keep working and praying. Every evening he and the boys went to the hospital to see Mary Ellen and pray together.

One afternoon at work, Barbara Rumble called and talked to Don Beachler. When Don hung up the phone, he said soberly, "Sheldon, they want you to go to the hospital right away because Mary Ellen is very low."

Don helped Sheldon into his car, and the two men headed for the hospital. They sped through the streets with Don driving as fast as could be expected in town with other traffic. Since it was mid-day, they made it in good time. Don wheeled Sheldon up to Mary Ellen's room. The Grover family was crying, surrounding the bed. The room felt strangely empty, as if someone had just left. Mary Ellen was partly upright with her hand up as if she were saying goodbye. Sheldon felt very calm as he looked and looked at the body of this woman who had been the other half of him, knowing that she was now with their Savior. Don wept with the rest of the family as they watched Sheldon silently observing his wife who had gone to be with her Lord.

Sheldon had tried to prepare himself for this moment, but nothing could compare with the grief he felt in this loss. The world looked different, and he was sure it would never be the same without Mary Ellen. It seemed like just yesterday he had been a strong young man who, with dreams of a bright future, looked into those pleading eyes. Eyes begging him to take her. Eyes that admired him. Eyes that loved him.

First it was his body that had abandoned him. Now he had lost his wife. Sheldon wept.

/ /

Mary Ellen was gone. It was September 13, 1971. The funeral was the first service the Modesto District had in their newly remodeled church building. It was hard to think that Sheldon would now need to raise two young boys by himself. Numbly, he went through the motions required of him even though he felt detached from the sights and sounds of life.

After the funeral was over, a minister approached Sheldon. Many of the members had left for their homes and the lunch was over.

"Sheldon," he said. "Now you're free to remarry if you would like."

Sheldon's head jerked back in shock before he was able to control his instinctive repulsion.

"Thank you for caring." His voice was clipped.

Later Sheldon related to Mark what the minister had said. He knew the minister's comment was well-intended, but it had hurt just the same.

"That made me very angry," said Sheldon. "I will never remarry. There was only one Mary Ellen, and besides, I've heard too many bad stories about situations with a stepmother and the children. It might work for some, but not for me."

Not only Sheldon was devastated with his wife's death; Harold, age 16, and Robert, age 10, were also shocked by the event. What child wouldn't be in shock when they saw their mother lowered in a casket into the ground? This was their mother. She had cared for them and loved them. Would life even be bearable? Could it possibly go on?

chapter twenty
"YET WILL I TRUST HIM"

1972

"It is difficult losing a loved one," said Sheldon, lifting himself up on his wheelchair with his elbows for a moment in a now-familiar movement to relieve the pressure in his hips. "But as Tennyson wrote, 'It's better to have loved and lost, than to have never loved at all.' "

He and his employer, Don Beachler, were having a heart-to-heart conversation, something that happened frequently when Don was also working in the office. Sometimes Don's responsibilities kept him out with the truck drivers. But today he was catching up on some of his own office work.

"I just don't know how it would be to lose Freeda," remarked Don thoughtfully. He shook his head. "I don't think I could go through that. You are so strong, Sheldon, and so calm."

Not only did Sheldon work at B&B Trucking with Don, but he also worked with Don in church work. They both served on the Modesto Church Charity Fund as well.

Sheldon was elected as the treasurer of the Fund, and Don was a member of the board. Since Don worked closely with Sheldon, he was often able to witness Sheldon's character of conscience and confidentiality.

He's the perfect Christian, Don mused as he considered Sheldon. Just the evening before, he and Freeda were talking about Sheldon's determination and quiet, stable way of contributing to life.

"It seems he never stops going. He is at the office like clockwork every morning and works all day without stopping so much as to take a break. I almost have to make him stop to get him to rest. I actually told him to figure his time straight through because he works non-stop." Don had scooted down on the couch and kicked his feet up on a stool. "If we all worked as hard as he does, we could do two or three times what we do now."

"I am glad he is working for you," Freeda's sweet voice had responded. "His presence is good for you and the employees."

The phone rang and Don answered it. Sheldon listened as his employer spoke with a driver. It sounded as if the driver had made a mistake somehow, and Don was scolding him for it. Sometimes the drivers didn't follow instructions well because they didn't know what was being explained. Other times drivers didn't follow instructions because they wanted to do it their way. Either way, the end result was often disaster.

"I've told you this many times before," barked Don and slammed down the phone.

"If only these guys would follow orders, life would be better," he grumbled.

A breeze gusted in the open office window and lifted a receipt from Don's desk. The paper fluttered to the floor and he grabbed it up with a disgruntled mutter. Beyond the window, a light rain had turned into a mist. A truck and trailer pulled up to the mechanic shop. The horn blew.

"Another driver have a question for you, Don?" Sheldon asked quietly. He arranged a stack of papers neatly, stood them upright, and tapped them on the desk. He laid them in the tray.

"Yeah. He just doesn't do what we tell him to do. I may need to lay him off."

"Whatever you decide, you need not speak quite so harshly, Don. We all make mistakes, and sometimes things are out of our control."

"But it creates all sorts of problems when they don't follow my instructions."

"I wonder what the Savior thinks when we don't follow His instructions?" Sheldon asked mildly.

"I guess I should have been a bit kinder in the way I spoke," Don sighed. "I suppose I can apologize when he comes back." He rubbed his forehead.

"Are there any matters pressing this afternoon, Don, or should I continue with the recording of receipts?" asked Sheldon softly.

The day passed as normal with workers coming and going, on schedule with their trucks. This particular day was a beehive of activity. The phone rang nearly all day with customers calling, pricing, and scheduling.

Near the close of day, Sam Bowers came into the office. Having left early in the morning to haul grain, he was ready to go home. He had been forced to wait most of the day at the place where he had offloaded his truck as that was company policy. Since it took some time for Don to line up a return load, Sam had to sit in his truck in the middle of nowhere, doing nothing.

"Wow, that was a long day," said Sam, wincing. "It feels like I drove halfway around the world." He rubbed his backside. "Boy, do I get tired of sitting."

He stopped short as he saw Sheldon looking at him in a peculiar way. He had forgotten about Sheldon at his spot behind the desk poring over his work without complaint.

"How are you doing today?" asked Sam.

"I am thankful I have the opportunity to work," Sheldon responded quietly. "Even if I need to sit all the time."

"Sorry," said Sam. He blushed deeply. "I shouldn't have been complaining. You have it much worse than I do."

"That's okay," replied Sheldon. "I understand. However, when I suffer it increases my desire and longing for when Christ comes again."

Soon the day was over, and Sheldon was driving home. He could hardly see to drive with his eyes blurring with tiredness. Surely he could make it a few miles home, and then he could lie down for a few minutes of rest.

"Daddy, what's for supper?" Robert's energetic voice greeted him as he pushed himself through the door.

Sheldon had just arrived home and was exhausted. Who wouldn't be tired after getting up at four o'clock in the morning to dress and prepare for the day? After making breakfast and seeing the boys off on the bus around seven-thirty, he too had left the house for his day at work. He had worked all day in the office and finally arrived home at five o'clock.

Nothing's for supper. Sheldon stared wearily at his son. *I haven't even thought about it yet.* He knew he needed to reassure Robert, so he responded.

"We will find something, Robert."

Deep within, Sheldon groaned. He would just have to shift gears and try to keep going. It was so difficult. He missed Mary Ellen. He had no clue what to make or even how to make it. He would have to pray as he always did about everything. Sheldon washed his hands at the deep sink and then wheeled into the kitchen, pausing to pray. *I can do all things through Christ which strengthens me. O God, help me know what to make and how to make it.*

It almost sounded like Mary Ellen's voice reverberating right through his mind as he paused. It seemed she was instructing him on a meal he could make for him and the boys. Taking down a worn cookbook, he quickly began finding the ingredients, calling for Harold or Robert to help him find what he needed. Soon a meal was cooked, and they sat down together to eat.

After the blessing, the boys dug in as if they hadn't had a decent meal for a couple of days.

"This is so good, Daddy. You're a good cook," exclaimed Robert.

Sheldon knew it was not through his own skills, but through the help of the Lord and Mary Ellen's voice in his mind that he had been able to make a meal.

Just then a truck drove in the lane, and Robert raced to the window to see who it was.

"It's Mark," he sang out. "He has a truck and trailer."

Mark was using one of the chicken houses as a place to store equipment for his landscaping business. Since the chicken houses were now empty, Sheldon had offered one of them as a shop for the business. "Might as well use them," said Sheldon. He was glad to offer the empty space to Mark for more than one reason. It would help Mark and his business, and keep him and his men close by, so they could stop in and see him from time to time. This was one key to his ability to endure all the pain and suffering—surround himself with people. He had lost one very dear relationship, and now he was determined to build more relationships around him.

"Whose turn to wash the dishes tonight?" asked Sheldon.

"It's Robert's turn," piped up Harold with a grin.

"No, it's not," retorted Robert. "It's yours. I did them this morning."

"Your memory's too good," grumbled the older brother. He put a few dishes into the sink, squirted some soap over them, and turned on the water.

As Sheldon prepared for bed that night, he was again struck at how empty his room was without Mary Ellen. He scooted from his wheelchair to his bed and worked his way into a comfortable position for the night. The long night. Sobs came slowly and then faster. He wept until tears came no more. He lay lonely and silent in the dark.

Mary Ellen was with the Lord, for which he was thankful, and someday he would see her again. But until then, he would need to keep focused, keep going, keep finding ways to be productive. He would never give up. He couldn't give up. He would trust in the sovereignty of God. He would do all things through Christ who strengthened him. He would endure, whether the threads being woven were light or dark.

He fell asleep and dreamed about gardens . . .

chapter twenty-one
TO GROW A GARDEN

1973

"Daddy." Robert was curious. "What in the world are you drawing?"

Robert had had enough of pencils, paper, and education, and wished he could help Mark on the landscaping business. He helped some in the summers and looked forward to helping more when he was out of school. But for now he knew he had to study. It was hard losing Mama. She had encouraged him with his schooling—and just about everything else.

Even though they did not have the wherewithal to buy everything they needed, much less what they wanted, Mama had somehow made sure they all felt loved and appreciated. She would make little gifts for Christmas or birthdays and sometimes just to surprise or encourage the family. He missed that.

She had also helped him with his school work if she knew the subject matter. One thing she wouldn't do though, no matter how much he would beg, was to tell the answer. "I will show you how to find the answer but I dare not tell it to you," she would say with a smile.

Now she was gone. Now he had only one parent. Despite his physical limitations, Daddy cared about him deeply.

"I am sketching a plan for the garden for this coming year," Sheldon absently answered his son's question, making another pencil line.

"Oh, no." Harold peered at the paper. "That means we will have to be planting garden soon. I thought you were drawing house plans." He groaned.

Sheldon chuckled. "No, I don't need a house. Look a little closer. Here are rows for beets, carrots, lettuce, potatoes, and radishes. I'll put a row of dahlias here to brighten the garden."

Before long the weather was warm enough to work up the garden. Mark came over with a plow to turn the soil. Then Harold tilled the garden and Robert helped him rake the soil out neatly and stretch out strings to make rows. So began an annual ministry of gardening and sharing produce that continued nearly to the end of Sheldon's life.

Sheldon would ride his electric cart and Harold and Robert would run back and forth as they prepared the garden according to the sketch their father had made. Sometimes Mark or the sons-in-law would stop in and also help with the preparation.

After the paths or aisles were made and packed for Sheldon's cart to drive on, someone would make furrows in the soil so Sheldon could start planting seeds. His inventive mind worked busily to find ways to adapt tools to fit his needs. He had a long one-inch pipe that he would use to plant the beans. He would drop a bean into the pipe, and it would slide all the way down and plop into the row right where he wanted it. When planting seedlings, he often needed assistance, but even then he would direct where they should be planted—always according to his sketch.

The garden was a project Sheldon enjoyed since it was something he could plan out ahead and then get his family to help him with. They joined him in soil preparation and then in harvesting, but as always, he wanted to do as much as possible by himself. He used his special tools to plant the seeds, then thin the rows and cut off small weeds. He used little sharp pieces of metal attached to the end of handles to cut off weeds or pick vegetables.

He would take long handles and fix hooks or knives on the end to grab objects far away or to cut weeds out of the flower beds or garden. *I can do it*, he thought. *I have to do it. There has to be a way.*

He also needed someone to help him lay down the irrigation lines and put up the sprinklers so that when the spring rains were over, he could water the growing garden.

It had been a year and a half since Mary Ellen had passed away, and Sheldon was learning how to deal with his loss and care for the boys. He prayed as he worked. How else could he keep going? *Lord, help me. Please help me,* he repeated over and over. *I don't know how to do this.* Then came his favorite verse. *I can do all things through Christ . . .*

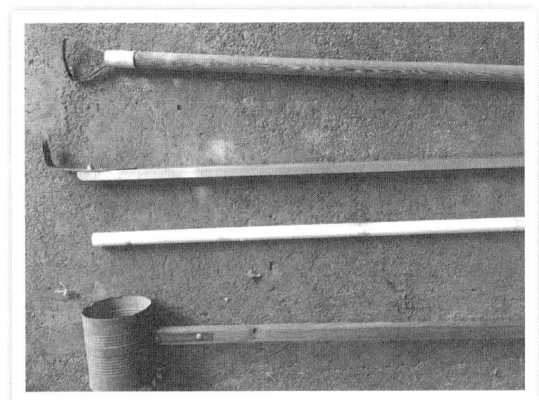

Some of Sheldon's gardening tools.

Filled with energy, courage, and determination, he slid from his cart back into this wheelchair. He tried to wheel himself up the ramp to the house, but he was just too tired. He would have to wait until one of the boys came back from putting his tools away.

He bowed his head. His hands hurt. His back hurt. Everything hurt, and now he would have to make something to eat.

As he waited, a vehicle pulled into the lane. He turned and looked. It was Flossie Rumble. What was she doing? He secretly hoped that she was bringing a meal for him and the boys. The Buick stopped and Flossie climbed out of the car.

"Hi, Sheldon. Just checking to see how the garden planting was going. Did you get the beans planted?"

She hadn't brought anything after all; just stopped to see how he and the boys were doing. He sighed.

"May I push you up the ramp?" she asked.

"I was waiting for one of the boys to come," he said. As he was speaking, Robert trudged up.

After Flossie checked out the garden, she was on her way. Harold and Robert came inside.

"What's for supper, Daddy?" asked Robert.

The phone rang, interrupting the question.

"Can you grab the phone, Harold?"

"It's Lorraine," said Harold putting the receiver to his chest. "She asked if we would like some macaroni and cheese for supper. She made plenty."

"Of course," said Sheldon. "Tell her to bring it down." He relaxed and bowed his head again to give thanks for the gift. Calls like these helped give him hope and strength.

Sometimes family or friends brought something by for Sheldon and the boys, which lightened Sheldon's load. But most of the time he and the boys had to fend for themselves.

He was glad that he was able to keep going. It was good for him to work, but it was indeed painful to sit so much. The only way to find relief was to lie down, something he just didn't have time for in his busy life of providing for himself and the boys.

It seemed as though he was constantly sitting: sitting in his wheelchair from morning to evening, sitting in his car to go to work, sitting at the office all day, and then sitting as he drove home. Then, once again, it was back to sitting in his wheelchair and electric cart. Sitting, sitting, sitting. *At least he could sit*, he thought. He was thankful he wasn't confined to a bed. He did get sores—of all his problems this bothered him the most—but he would just try to ignore the pain and go on.

His garden gave him something to look forward to in the evenings after work and on Saturdays. He knew his garden from one end to the other. He knew every plant and how it looked and how it was progressing. He knew how each kind of leaf was supposed to look and knew if it had been molested by a bug. The garden was his life. It was another reason to live.

But surely there were other things he could do to keep his mind off his limitations and losses. *How would it be to travel?* Sheldon wondered longingly. He knew it wouldn't be easy since access to places of interest, other homes, and restrooms were not built with his needs in mind. But he felt sure he could learn to manage these challenges, just as he had learned to manage all the rest of life, with determination and endurance.

Sheldon's garden.

chapter twenty-two
BEYOND THE SIERRAS

1974

Autumn, 1974. It was a year to remember in the United States. The Super Outbreak of tornadoes across parts of the Midwest had killed 319 people. The country had experienced the worst stock market crash since the Great Depression, as well as the resigning of President Nixon because of the Watergate scandal.

Gasoline had to be rationed across the states since the Middle East had placed an embargo on oil sold to the United States and a few other countries. To help decrease consumption, a national maximum speed limit of 55 mph was enforced through the Emergency Highway Energy Conservation Act that year. In some states, gas stations were limiting the amount of fuel each vehicle could buy or closing down completely.

Those who wanted to travel found ways to overcome the challenge. Some figured out beforehand where the gas stations were. Others simply allowed more time in their driving, and still others traveled through areas that didn't impose such stiff gasoline restrictions.

Sheldon continued to explore the possibilities of someday traveling somewhere beyond the mountains. But where? And when? He wouldn't have long to wait, it turned out.

"What do you think about going on a trip with us to Kansas?" asked Mark in early November. "We have been thinking of going to Roger and Janice's wedding." Mark watched Sheldon's reaction and continued.

"Why don't you and Harold and Robert go along too," he proposed. "We'll plan on taking your station wagon since that's what you're used to driving."

"I would like that." Sheldon's grin spread across his face. "I have never been out of California yet, so maybe this would be my chance."

So after researching the route and making plans with acquaintances, they began packing their suitcases. Harold decided to stay at home to keep ahead of his studies in college. Sheldon and Robert would go along on the trip with Mark, Lorraine, and the boys.

"Do you know how old I am today?" asked Peter as the car load headed out of Modesto. He eyed Sheldon suspiciously. "Did Mama tell you?"

"No, she didn't," replied Sheldon. He grinned at his lively grandson. "Let me guess. You are seven years old."

"How did you know?" He raised his voice. "Mama, did you tell Grandpa?"

"Not today," replied Lorraine. "Grandpa already knows when you were born so he simply calculated."

Along the way, the travelers stopped for some ice cream to celebrate Peter's birthday. Sheldon would soon be fifty-three years old; though he might have lacked Peter's boyish exuberance, he too was excited. He was looking forward to the trip across the western United States, and he silently prayed for a safe and enjoyable trip. Tule fog covered the San Joaquin Valley as the Grovers motored toward Bakersville. The station wagon's tires hummed as they met the pavement while the occupants sang inside. As they drove through southern California, they were able to see a variety of desert life. Sheldon especially enjoyed the Joshua Cactus trees along the highway.

The travelers' first destination was the White Sands National Monument in New Mexico. They drove partway the first day before stopping for the night. They hoped to drive the remaining distance the next day and arrive at their destination before it got too late. That is, if they could find gas stations with fuel.

For Sheldon's sake, they wanted to make the trip worthwhile, knowing that it might be his first and last trip out of state. They would take the southern route on the way to Kansas.

Before leaving for the trip, Sheldon had gathered information about the White Sands area. Spanish explorers and miners had come to the area for salt and gypsum. The U.S. military had also used the large expanse of white sand for scientific research and had tested the first atom bomb here in 1945.

They spent the morning at White Sands National Monument which had a visitor center and of course the famous white sand dunes as far as the eye could see. Mark and Lorraine ran up and down the vast sea of snow-white gypsum dunes with Peter, Adam, and Robert. Sheldon sat in his wheelchair and observed the shimmering whiteness, the dry smell of sand, and the whistling desert winds.

Then they drove on to the Carlsbad Caverns in the Chihuahuan Desert, also of southern New Mexico. This too was a memorable stop for Sheldon. The largest room of the caverns was wheelchair accessible so he was able to see for himself the splendor of this underground drama. He noted the giant conglomeration of spectacular rocks that was named "Rock of Ages"—but thought it paled considerably when compared to the Rock of Ages he knew.

He noted the differences between the flora and fauna of southern New Mexico and that of their home area back in Modesto. Desert fauna and flora had to survive on much less moisture than those found in his own area, where an average of thirteen inches of rain fell each year.

The travelers arrived in Quinter, Kansas, in good time to recover from the trip and visit family and friends before the wedding. Their friends Calvin and Ethel were gracious enough to let them stay at their house for almost a week. Sheldon appreciated learning to know family that he had never met before. Many of his relatives had already heard his story from others who had visited him in California. At least this saved him a lot of explanation.

Sheldon thoroughly enjoyed his time with the brothers and sisters from these Mid-western German Baptist communities. It was an eye-opener to see the unique issues that they were dealing with in their community in comparison to those in Modesto. However, many of the problems these dear friends faced were the same ones they faced in California. *It appears that people are the same the world around,* he mused. What had Job observed? *Yet man is born unto trouble, as the sparks fly upward.*[1]

After nearly three weeks of visiting in various homes and sight-seeing, Sheldon was ready to go back to California—home. Now he had more friends who knew him better and who promised to pray for him. This too gave him courage to keep pressing on in his daily suffering. Sometimes his adversity was hard to understand, let alone bear, but with continual support from brothers and sisters far and wide, he could and would be faithful. After all, Jesus suffered much more physical abuse and shame than he ever would. If Jesus could endure so much suffering—and suffering He didn't even deserve—then surely Sheldon could endure what he had to suffer.

A cold wind was chilling the Midwest as the travelers loaded their luggage for the trip home. Mark walked around the station wagon and kicked the tires to be sure they were okay. Lorraine checked the bedrooms for articles they might have forgotten. Sheldon mentally went over his checklist of things he didn't want to leave behind, and the boys ran to climb a Kansas tree for the last time before they were stuck in the station wagon for many hours.

They decided to take the northern route home and stop at Hoover Dam and Zion National Park. Taking this route would allow Sheldon to see the states of Utah and Nevada.

As the scenery slid by, Sheldon thought longingly about Mary Ellen and the many good memories they had made together. It would be so nice to have her along on this trip, so she could enjoy it with him. But regardless of how much he wished it, the possibility was over. His life with her was past.

---

[1] Job 5:7

Although he had wonderful memories of the experiences they had together, he had to guard his thoughts lest he become discouraged. He would meet her again. Someday. Perhaps today! Wouldn't that be great to meet her in the sky or in the new kingdom?

chapter twenty-three
FIRST IN WORSHIP

2000

Sheldon grabbed the knotted ropes that were tied to the frame above his bed and pulled himself up. He rolled to the side and grabbed the side ropes. The frame and knotted ropes had been built and installed so he could shift himself or get to the edge of the bed. He edged closer to the stand and shut off the blaring alarm clock.

He prayed for strength. He needed to get up. He wanted to get up. Even though it was tough to get out of bed, he was always determined to get up early and dress himself, to be well groomed before starting his day. Today it would take him even longer than normal, and he would need to rise earlier than usual. *Even before the crowing of the cock*, he thought wryly. But today was a special day, and he wouldn't dare oversleep.

Sheldon scooted into his wheelchair, wheeled to the closet, and pulled down his white dress shirt and black pants. Now for the challenge of getting them on. He had gone through this morning procedure hundreds of times and it never got easier. In his mind he wanted to shout and scream, but outwardly he was calm. He wanted to slip into his clothing just as he had done when he was a boy and dash out the door like an Indian, but that would never happen again. He wheeled back to his bed where he would shift and squirm and wiggle until he was dressed.

After he was dressed, he picked up his Bible and wheeled to the living room to study and pray. This was an important part of his day. He longed to become more like his Savior. He was looking forward to the morning service too.

Today was the Lord's Day and he wanted to be on time. He could not be late. He would be first and he would be up front. The Lord was worthy of the effort it took to accomplish this.

Soon Robert was already up and getting dressed, so Sheldon started breakfast. As he worked, he prayed that God would help him with the food preparation.

"Daddy, can I help you somehow?" asked Robert. "Should I put something on to drink? A cup of hot tea?"

"Oh, good morning, son. Yes, that would be good." Sheldon tried to flip an egg but got it turned only halfway. The yoke ran sizzling across the pan.

Sheldon's neck and arm were in pain as he finished putting on the food. He pushed himself to his place at the table. Father and son ate, making occasional small talk.

"Did you see Aunt Frieda recently, Robert?" Sheldon scooted back from the table.

"Saw her this week."

Sheldon brushed a few crumbs off his pants. "I heard she wants to get her house paid off soon. Pop said something about it."

Sheldon wished he could do something more for his sister. Perhaps he could send her a bit more money this month to help with the mortgage. Maybe it was true that he couldn't afford to give much more, but what he could give, he would.

After Robert had washed the dishes, they relaxed a few minutes before heading out to the car. It was early, but Sheldon was determined to be in plenty of time. He didn't mind being the first person in at church. It was common for him to be in the sanctuary at his usual spot in the front before anyone else arrived.

"Good morning, Howard," greeted Sheldon. "How are you?"

"I am well, thank you," replied Howard Flory, his friend from his younger years. "It sure is a beautiful Lord's day, isn't it?"

"A beautiful day for the Lord to come again," Sheldon affirmed.

"Every day would be a beautiful day for the Lord to come again." Howard scooted into a pew and got settled in.

One of the deacons led a song that morning that touched Sheldon's soul. Later, he tried to recall the words. "The cross that He gave may be heavy, but it ne'er outweighs His grace. The storm that I feared may surround me, but it ne'er excludes His face."[1]

After a few years had passed, Sheldon was able to upgrade from his manual wheelchair to a motorized one. A van was also purchased to accommodate the newer, larger wheelchair.

One Sunday morning after his normal routine of dressing, personal worship, and breakfast, he decided to drive to church on his motorized wheelchair. This was easier to do now that all the children were married and he had only himself to worry about. He left early so he could enjoy the ride.

He savored the beauty of spring in Modesto with flowerbeds well-tended and new tree growth bursting. A variety of palm and eucalyptus trees were sprinkled between houses and the quiet backstreets that bordered them. A giant oak tree guarded the north side of Rumble Road.

Times had sure changed since he was a boy. He remembered all of this land open and stretching across the valley. Most of Modesto had been to the south, but now it had grown in all directions. Houses, stores, and malls were constructed where once there was virgin soil.

A dove's mournful call stirred Sheldon's emotions with memories of days

---

[1] *The Cross That He Gave May Be Heavy*, Ballington Booth

gone by when he had lived on Shoemake Avenue with Pop and Mama. A car passed. It was Rodney and Marilyn. They too were headed for church. His grandson Matt and wife were walking to church, so they joined him.

As Sheldon approached Lou Ann Drive, he checked for cars. Since he didn't hear or see any, he gave his wheelchair a bit of forward speed. Too late, he realized he had not lined up his wheels correctly with the little sidewalk ramp that tapered down to the street. Since the left tire was still running up on the sidewalk, it kicked him and his motorized cart sideways and over onto the road. With a thud Sheldon landed, his cart lying on its side behind him.

"Grandpa," hollered Matt in alarm. Annie shrieked.

Sheldon groaned. His face and hands were bleeding and he could not turn over to get up. *Now look at me,* Sheldon thought wretchedly. *Lying on the road with no way to get up by myself, much less get the wheelchair back upright and get into it. I'm no better than a turtle upended on its shell!* His chest heaved with bitter sobs.

"Are you okay?" Matt knelt by his side. "It happened so fast. Let me help you sit up."

"Oh God," Sheldon prayed desperately. "Help me." He had a stabbing pain in his left leg. He didn't know where the pain was worst; he hurt everywhere. Tears came to his eyes.

Just then Sheldon heard a car slow and stop. He heard the door being shoved open.

"Matt! Sheldon! Are you okay?" The welcome voice came from John Fall, also on his way to church.

Matt and John were able to help Sheldon to a more comfortable position.

"I'm going to be late for church," groaned Sheldon.

"I don't think you'll be going to church today, Grandpa. We need to get you fixed up."

Sheldon moaned. Missing church would be worse than a bleeding face and hands.

Soon more help arrived and Sheldon was carried to a vehicle and taken to the hospital where he rested a few days. His leg was broken and had to be set and put into a splint.

Doctor Shirk was about to release Sheldon to go home. He tugged at his goatee and smiled. His teeth shone an impressive white as he chuckled widely.

"Don't be diving out of your wheelchair again, you hear? You're getting too old for stunts like these."

"No, I don't plan to dive out of my wheelchair again," Sheldon responded with embarrassment. "And by the way, accidents aren't planned. But now I need to get to my garden before it dries up."

chapter twenty-four
ACCIDENTS AREN'T PLANNED

2000–2001

Sheldon gazed thoughtfully at the bonsai tree in front of him. He was wearing a gardener's hat to keep the beating sun from scorching his head, and he whistled a tune as he trained his miniature trees. The small saplings that he pruned and trained helped him fulfill his desire to work with trees and observe God's orderly world. Perhaps *he* was one of God's bonsai trees which needed continued pruning and training.

Since he couldn't work in orchards and vineyards, he would work with bonsai trees. He had learned that it was a Japanese art originating from the Chinese several thousand years earlier. The art of pruning roots and branches to produce a tiny tree with the same features as a large one was relaxing to Sheldon.

As Sheldon worked outdoors, he felt the presence and pleasure of God. He was occupied in God's world and this brought him joy. Flowers were also a part of this joy, and his specialty was growing miniature roses and Gerbera

A typical scene, Sheldon coming from the garden on his motorized wheelchair.

daisies. He cared for his garden, plants, trees, and flowers with the passion of a large spirit forced into a confined expression. He still had the inner energy of an active man, but was forced to channel it into a narrow focus to accomplish such small things. Able-bodied men dressed themselves almost without thought, yet he spent more than an hour to achieve the result that took them minutes. *Maybe that's why I enjoy the bonsai tree work*, he thought.

He was indebted to Phil Layman for building wooden counters around the outside of his apartment. The counters had been constructed at the proper height for Sheldon to access his tree and flower pots.

Sheldon was also glad that Harold and Becky had agreed to buy the home place. They would live in the house, and the egg room would be converted into living quarters for him.

The egg room was remodeled into a beautiful little house just right for one person. Some of the brothers had installed lowered cabinets and tables and closets and drawers for easier access. Gary Miller and a few brothers from church had also installed an indoor pool for him to relax and bathe in to relieve his muscle and skin pain.

Recalling Gary, he had to chuckle. He liked Gary. He was funny but could also be serious. What was Gary's remark about growing a tail like a fish if he swam too much in the pool? *People are fun*, he thought. Even if some people were unhandy or quite a pain, they still were people. He enjoyed different personalities and tastes just like he enjoyed different foods.

But one thing he didn't enjoy was accidents. Perhaps this dislike had resulted from the trauma of losing his mobility with polio. He had always been one to take risks but now that he was handicapped it did make him more vulnerable.

Sheldon thought now of the accident he had experienced recently. Even though it was a warm day in the sun, he chilled thinking of how close he had come to drowning in the pool. It had been a near-fatal accident.

A hoist had been installed for him to use in accessing the pool. It was installed on a track that ran above his bed and all the way into the next room where the pool had been built. He would undress and scoot into the hoist with straps under his flaccid arms and legs. Then by operating a hand held device, he would use the electric hoist to drop himself down into a chair that had been fastened to the floor of the pool.

He recalled the chair being a bit slick. His body, with its added age and weight, became more top-heavy and buoyant. When he had tried to get out of his hoist and into his chair, he slipped and almost fell headlong into the pool.

He shuddered again, remembering the close call. If he would have fallen, he wouldn't have been able, with his mouth and lungs filled with water, to shout for help. He had grabbed wildly for the chair and the hoist and, fortunately, he had managed to right himself. From then on he called his son-in-law Harold from the adjoining house to be with him when he went to soak.

Sheldon was thankful for Harold's help. He was very glad that Harold had married into the family. God must have known that he needed someone so patient to look after him when he was feeble. He chuckled as he thought about his sons Mark and Harold who had tried to put his compression socks on when son-in-law Harold was away for several weeks. Whew. They just didn't have the patience to work those socks up into place. Once when Mark took them off, he just grabbed the top and jerked them down and off as hard as he could. He chuckled even harder at the memory. He almost flew out of his chair and the socks—poor things—had runners and looked pitiful.

Sheldon snipped another branch. There. It looked just right. He checked the irrigation lines that ran to each pot.

Next, he wanted to take a drive around the property.

Sometimes Sheldon simply drove around his property and checked out the trees and shrubs so that he could tell Harold Long which ones needed care. If he was able, he did the work by himself. After Mary Ellen's death, he had planted grapevines and fruit trees. He chose peach, pluot, apricot, plum, and persimmon trees; a number of walnut trees had already been planted before he bought the property.

As Sheldon checked the trees and pulled weeds here and there, he happened to drive near a hole where a tree had been taken out. Harold Long had dug up a tree but had not yet replanted one, and a big hole remained. The edges were soft and as Sheldon drove by too closely, his motorized wheelchair started tipping. He tried to lean back, but it was too late. He and his wheelchair were pitched into the hole.

Sheldon shouted for help. Since Harold was at work and Becky was inside the house, no one came to his rescue. "Oh God, please help me," he said. He was in a painful position. *At least the soil is dry and soft*, he thought. He continued to shout but now he became aware of another problem. He was getting weak from shouting and from trying to maintain his crumpled position.

Suddenly, he heard a voice coming from behind the nearby fence. It was the neighbor girl who lived on the street behind them. He had never liked the way she acted or dressed, so in his mind he had named her Jezebel. But now here she was, coming to his rescue.

"I'll run get help, sir," the girl called over the fence. Sheldon heard her feet crunching gravel and weeds as she ran to get help. He waited until he gave up hope of anyone coming to help him. *O Lord, what can I do? You are my only Source of help.*

After what seemed an age, several men from Vintage Pools, a business next door, hurried over.

"Hey, Sheldon. We heard you got into trouble." They carefully pulled him and his wheelchair out of the dip in the ground.

"Thanks," said Sheldon as he tried to spit the dirt out of his mouth. "I didn't know if anyone would show up or not."

"Yeah, your neighbor came over and told us," they explained.

So she had told someone, thought Sheldon. He brushed the dirt off his pants the best he could and tried out his motorized wheelchair to see if it still worked. It jerked ahead. Good. He could drive back to his apartment. He would have to be more careful where he drove.

Another day, Sheldon was in his lush green garden trying to adjust the Rainbird sprinkler with his handle and hook. Somehow, in the process, he got off the path into the soft soil near the tomatoes and his chair got stuck. The sprinkler was on, and each time it came around it soaked him.

"What should I do now," mumbled Sheldon under his breath. "Another crazy accident." He hadn't planned for this; otherwise, he would have worn a raincoat and boots. The water streaming down around his wheelchair wasn't doing anything to improve the condition of the soil.

Becky and Harold L., as they often called his son-in-law, were not at home. He couldn't cry out to them for help. He was glad that he carried his cordless phone with him, but he knew he had better call quickly before the constant water would drain the battery. He dialed Grover Landscaping. Maybe he could get help there.

Water was dripping off Sheldon's face and arms. Every time the sprinkler made its round, he braced himself for another hit. Again his helplessness was brought home to him. *I'm a cripple,* he thought grimly. *I can have all the energy and ideas I want inside, but this twisted frame of mine limits me so much. O God,* he prayed, *help me to humble my independent spirit and accept help when I need it.*

In a few minutes, Sheldon heard the high-pitched whine of an engine as a vehicle flew up Rumble Road. Maybe this was his rescuer. Sure enough, the vehicle skidded in the lane and he heard a siren. "Oh no, don't tell me someone called emergency services," Sheldon grunted. *How humiliating!*

A white Ford pickup skidded to a halt, his son Harold leaning out the window making the sound of a siren with his mouth and laughing. Sheldon simply shook his head as water dripped off of him, and Harold ran to shut off the water.

"Got yourself in another fix, did you, Daddy?"

"Got off the edge of the path as I was trying to adjust the sprinkler." Sheldon tried not to grumble.

"A rather one-sided water fight, I'd say," Harold said as he helped push the wheelchair back. Sheldon shoved the lever into reverse.

That evening Becky and Harold L. made a special meal of grilled fish and fresh apple pie for Sheldon.

"Sorry we weren't here to help you," said Becky. She smiled as Sheldon described how Harold had driven into the lane mimicking a siren.

"It keeps life interesting," admitted Harold L. He secretly wished he could have seen the sight, but the story was good enough. No one knew how long Sheldon would be around yet, and they all wanted to make the best of the time they had together.

chapter twenty-five
"WILL THE CIRCLE BE UNBROKEN?"

2001–2009

"Perhaps today!" thought Sheldon as he drove his motorized wheelchair out to his garden. He looked forward each day to the Second Coming. Soon he would be a part of the New Jerusalem coming down out of heaven adorned as a bride for her husband.

He checked the corn. It was ready.

Each spring Sheldon drew his garden sketch, comparing the new sketch with the previous year's. He double checked to be sure the crops were rotated properly. Then when the weather was consistent for planting, he called the family together.

The potatoes were planted the first part of February after the garden was plowed. Each fall, after all the produce was harvested, Sheldon planted a cover crop. Eventually the soil became so alive with microbiology and fertility that he was able to produce a dark green garden without commercial fertilizer.

In mid-June, after the beets, carrots, lettuce, potatoes, radishes and many other crops were harvested, Sheldon would plant half of the garden with sweet corn. Again, after someone had prepared the soil and dug furrows, he would plant the corn seeds, dropping them one at a time through his long one-inch pipe.

The family helped him prepare the garden, plant some of the seeds, and lay out the irrigation. From there, Sheldon managed the garden himself. When the produce was mature, he would let Harold L. and Becky know and then call Rodney, Mark, Harold, and Robert's families. He would insist that they stop in and pull a few radishes or pick a few tomatoes or whatever else was ripe. It was a labor of love from a daddy to his children and grandchildren.

Sometimes during the day, Sheldon would not have a lunch but simply go out to his garden, pick up a vegetable or two, and eat it fresh. That was the best way to eat vegetables anyway. Fresh.

All his work in the garden was done from his electric egg cart or his motorized "garden" wheelchair on the packed pathways that Harold L. or one of his sons had made for him with the roto-tiller.

When the corn was ready in the fall, Sheldon let the family know and they planned a corn day. The menfolk got together at the garden and picked the corn. Then they shucked it and left the husks lying in the garden for compost.

"That's easier than hauling it off somewhere else anyway," said Harold with a grin.

The shucked corn was taken over to Harold and Pam's place since they had a garage that was suitable for doing the remaining work. Large burners heated the water in big kettles.

The ladies blanched the corn in hot water for a few minutes before dipping it out with large sieves and dumping it into the cool water. The children and grandchildren helped move the corn from tub to tub of cool water and then to ice water to rapidly cool the blanched corn.

"Stay back from the hot water," Pam said. She shooed some of the little ones away from the heated water. "We don't need anyone getting scalded."

Sheldon wheeled back and forth, helping where most needed. This was one thing he lived for; working together with his children and grandchildren.

While Sheldon worked, he also prayed. He loved each one and was concerned for them and the choices they were making.

The men cut the cooled corn off the cob while they talked about the latest news. This was always a special day for everyone.

The garden was a way to bless his family and to show his love and appreciation for them. It was also a way to keep their circle together.

Sheldon continued to pray for his children and grandchildren each day when he arose for his time of worship. He wasn't always comfortable with all the choices his children and grandchildren were making, but he knew each one was created with the ability to choose as he pleased.

It was especially difficult when news reached him of his grandson Peter's death. Working for Grover Landscaping one day, Peter had been rappelling out of a large oak tree on the Rumble Ranch close to the Stanislaus River when, about halfway down, his heart suddenly stopped beating. He died almost instantly. Dustin, another one of Grover Landscaping's tree climbers, was with him. He had called 911, and then climbed up and brought Peter down and started CPR until the firemen and ambulance came. But it had been no use. Peter, an athletic young father at age 32, was gone.

As Sheldon wheeled close to the casket, tears streamed down his face, creased and seamed with years of suffering. He gazed at the still form which only a few days before had been filled with energy and life.

"This should be me instead of Peter." Sheldon choked with emotion. "I'm old and in a wheelchair and Mary Ellen is gone and I would like to go, and Peter was so young and left behind a beautiful wife and two precious children." *Why, God? Why?*

Sheldon's pain subsided slightly as he recalled his great-grandson Andrew standing beside the casket and looking at Peter's body, saying, "Grandpa, I wish Jesus would come and raise him." *Don't we all wish that,* thought Sheldon. He carried the grief of that loss for a long time.

The verse he carried so near his heart all these years came back again in a flash. "And we know that all things work together for good to them that love God, to them who are the called according to his purpose." He would have to trust that God's way is perfect and that the Judge of all the earth will do right.

Sheldon sighed. He had been in a wheelchair longer now than he had been out of one. Sadly, he also realized he had lived more years without Mary Ellen than the years they had been together as husband and wife. Some memories were dim, but some were still as clear as the day he had experienced them.

He drove outside on his wheelchair; a strong man, enduring alone.

The end.

EPILOGUE

After retiring from B&B Trucking, Sheldon worked at home with his bonsai trees and fruit and nut trees, flowers, and gardening. Sheldon's daughter Rebecca and her husband Harold Long bought the home place and cared for Sheldon in his sunset years.

Up until his passing Sheldon was treasurer of the Modesto District Fund and faithfully and discreetly handled contributions and passed them on to those in need.

Family, friends, and fellow employees were emphatic with their statements regarding Sheldon's character and life habits. He was faithful, consistent, predictable and Christ-like. I am sure that if I would have had the opportunity to speak to Sheldon directly, he would have shared insight into areas of his life that needed growth. However, the testimonies of those who knew him reveal a man of depth, a man who was quiet but able to make a person feel loved, respected, and appreciated by a listening ear and gentle advice. Perhaps it could be said of Sheldon as it was of Abel . . . by faith he still speaks, even though he is dead.

During the winter of 2008-2009 he became increasingly weak. He was diagnosed as being dehydrated and taken to Memorial Medical Center Emergency Room February 5, 2009, where it was discovered that he also had pneumonia. Very soon he began the peaceful passing from time to eternity. Sheldon passed from wheelchairs, weakness, and misery, and into eternity on February 8, 2009.

At the date of his death, his children Mark and Lorraine Grover, Marilyn and Rodney Gish, Rebecca and Harold Long, Harold and Pamela Grover, and Robert and Suzie Grover survived. All of them lived in Modesto. Fourteen grandchildren, 16 great grandchildren, and many nieces and nephews, cousins, and friends also survive.

Sheldon Grover, shortly before he died.

ABOUT THE AUTHOR

Harold Troyer lives in the charming village of Belleville in the Kishacoquillas Valley of central Pennsylvania. He, his Ukrainian wife Larissa, and six children love singing, traveling, and gardening. Harold taught junior high students for six years, bounced on a bus through Nicaragua's interior, navigated the muddy rivers of Papua New Guinea in a dugout, and stood in an unending sea of waving wheat in Ukraine. All these adventures have provided contexts for his passionate study of anthropology.

Harold has served as a foreign missionary in Central America and Eastern Europe, and has been involved in prison ministry and aftercare in the United States. Currently he serves on the Board of Directors for All-Nations Bible Translation, is a phone team member in CAM's Billboard Evangelism Program, and has a sideline construction business.

Harold desires that readers would turn their eyes on Jesus and journey further with God by reading about men and women who have fought the good fight of faith. Harold would like reader comments on his book, which can be sent to htroyer@camoh.org. or by writing Christian Aid Ministries at P.O. Box 360, Berlin, OH 44610, Attn: Harold Troyer.

ABOUT CHRISTIAN AID MINISTRIES

Christian Aid Ministries was founded in 1981 as a nonprofit, tax-exempt 501(c)(3) organization. Its primary purpose is to provide a trustworthy and efficient channel for Amish, Mennonite, and other conservative Anabaptist groups and individuals to minister to physical and spiritual needs around the world. This is in response to the command to ". . . do good unto all men, especially unto them who are of the household of faith" (Galatians 6:10).

Each year, CAM supporters provide 15–20 million pounds of food, clothing, medicines, seeds, Bibles, Bible story books, and other Christian literature for needy people. Most of the aid goes to orphans and Christian families. Supporters' funds also help to clean up and rebuild for natural disaster victims, put up Gospel billboards in the U.S., support several church-planting efforts, operate two medical clinics, and provide resources for needy families to make their own living. CAM's main purposes for providing aid are to help and encourage God's people and bring the Gospel to a lost and dying world.

CAM has staff, warehouses, and distribution networks in Romania,

Moldova, Ukraine, Haiti, Nicaragua, Liberia, Israel, and Kenya. Aside from management, supervisory personnel, and bookkeeping operations, volunteers do most of the work at CAM locations. Each year, volunteers at our warehouses, field bases, Disaster Response Services projects, and other locations donate over 200,000 hours of work.

CAM's ultimate purpose is to glorify God and help enlarge His kingdom. ". . . whatsoever ye do, do all to the glory of God" (1 Corinthians 10:31).

THE WAY TO GOD AND PEACE

We live in a world contaminated by sin. Sin is anything that goes against God's holy standards. When we do not follow the guidelines that God our Creator gave us, we are guilty of sin. Sin separates us from God, the source of life.

Since the time when the first man and woman, Adam and Eve, sinned in the Garden of Eden, sin has been universal. The Bible says that we all have "sinned and come short of the glory of God" (Romans 3:23). It also says that the natural consequence for that sin is eternal death, or punishment in an eternal hell: "Then when lust hath conceived, it bringeth forth sin: and sin, when it is finished, bringeth forth death" (James 1:15).

But we do not have to suffer eternal death in hell. God provided forgiveness for our sins through the death of His only Son, Jesus Christ. Because Jesus was perfect and without sin, He could die in our place. "For God so loved the world that he gave his only begotten Son, that whosoever believeth in him should not perish, but have everlasting life" (John 3:16).

A sacrifice is something given to benefit someone else. It costs the giver greatly. Jesus was God's sacrifice. Jesus' death takes away the penalty of sin for all those who accept this sacrifice and truly repent of their sins. To repent of sins means to be truly sorry for and turn away from the things we have done that have violated God's standards (Acts 2:38; 3:19).

Jesus died, but He did not remain dead. After three days, God's Spirit miraculously raised Him to life again. God's Spirit does something similar in us. When we receive Jesus as our sacrifice and repent of our sins, our hearts are changed. We become spiritually alive! We develop new desires and attitudes (2 Corinthians 5:17). We begin to make choices that please God (1 John 3:9). If we do fail and commit sins, we can ask God for forgiveness. "If we confess our sins, he is faithful and just to forgive us our sins, and to cleanse us from all unrighteousness" (1 John 1:9).

Once our hearts have been changed, we want to continue growing spiritually. We will be happy to let Jesus be the Master of our lives and will want to become more like Him. To do this, we must meditate on God's Word and commune with God in prayer. We will testify to others of this change by being baptized and sharing the good news of God's victory over sin and death. Fellowship with a faithful group of believers will strengthen our walk with God (1 John 1:7).